The Winter of Magical Letters

The Winter of Magical Letters

Written and Illustrated by
Elizabeth Dye

Seven Arches
Publishing

Published in July 2009
By Seven Arches Publishing
27, Church Street, Nassington, Peterborough PE8 61QG
www.sevenarchespublishing.co.uk

A catalogue record for this book is available from the British Library

Graphics by Alan McGlynn

Printed in Great Britain by imprintdigital.net

ISBN 978-0-9556169-5-2

To Gabriel who loves science and Amelia who loves words.

Chapter 1

The Shining Letters

Glittering and gleaming, it lay there amongst the dead leaves. When Sam had found the first of the scraps of paper, he had almost kicked it aside, and had only bent down to pick it up because it was so strange. One side was plain white, but the other was patterned with hexagons, all shining like mother-of-pearl with a faint sparkle to the colours, as if each shape had been dipped in stardust. He didn't even notice what was written on the back.

Just a slip of paper, but somehow odd. Sam shoved it into his pocket, and continued scuffling up the brown leaves.

When school had been particularly bad, he would walk home through his special wood where he could forget that he was small; the smallest boy in his class – no, worse – the smallest *child* in his class; he was even smaller than Jessie Brown, and as if that wasn't enough he had bright red hair. In amongst the tangled tree trunks there was nobody to notice him. Best of all, there was no Toughie Wilson to jeer or terrorise, to bully or torment him.

That night in bed, in the tiny cupboard of a bedroom, which his grandmother kept for him, he remembered the scrap of paper and stretched his hand out of the covers to reach into his anorak pocket. The bedroom was so small he could touch each wall. The ceiling was deep blue, dotted with gold stars. He had a real fur cover on his bed, and the curtains were embroidered to look like forest leaves. It was a hideaway.

The scrap of paper looked just as extraordinary by lamplight, and the patterns seemed to shift a little. Looking at it, Sam felt a tingle inside. It was only while he was folding it up that he noticed the letters written on the back. In big bold handwriting were:

Be Mg Ca Sr Ba Ra

Now the tiny tingle that had been there inside him was a quiver, shivering down his backbone. He sat for a long time looking at the weird combination of letters, **Be Mg Ca Sr Ba Ra**. What did they mean? Someone's name? A coded message? A foreign language? The password for a computer?

Even, perhaps, magic letters! If only they were just that: magic letters!

Sam stretched down, one arm groping under the bed for the place where he kept his treasures. Right at the back was a small brightly painted box; his own private treasure box. The outside showed a young man and a girl, coloured in pinks and greens and yellows. Written on the inside of the lid, in gold lettering, were the words ' to J.R. from K.X'. He didn't know who J.R. or K.X. had been. They were just part of the mystery of his secret box. In it were his very special cards. They were his most treasured possessions. He folded the paper carefully and placed it on top of the cards, safe inside the box.

He was sleepy. Tomorrow he would work it out. He switched on the disc player. Earlier that evening his grandmother had said, "I'm taking your music education in hand. I want you to listen to this tonight."

"Oh Gran! Boring Granny stuff! What is it anyhow?"

" 'Night on a Bare Mountain'! And it's about as boring as skate-boarding down Everest."

He was surprised, because he had never noticed his grandmother listening to music. So why was she suddenly taking an interest in what he listened to?

The letters swirled around his head, the music rose and fell, and he drifted off to sleep and dreamed.

What a dream! There was **Be**ryl the **M**agnificent **str**iding to and fro, **ca**lling and calling, her voice bouncing off the walls, till up ran the **Sr**angle **ba**rking loudly and **ra**pidly, and he was in the middle, spinning and turning, trapped by **Be**ryl the **M**agnificent **C**alling the **Sr**angles **Ba**rking **Ra**pidly!

Next morning Sam remembered **Be Mg Ca Sr Ba Ra**. How did those odd letters fall into his dream - that weird dream of the **Magnificent Beryl calling** up the **ra**pidly **bar**king **Sr**angles?

At breakfast he told his grandmother all about the strangely beautiful paper with its odd letters, and how his dream had echoed the very same letters.

"Sam, what is a Srangle?" she asked.

"You know, Gran, you know a Srangle."

"No I don't! What does it look like?" He gazed back into his dream, just to make sure he got the Srangle exactly right.

And it was at that point that he realized that he didn't know what a Srangle was either. One moment he had known exactly what it was and the next moment the whole picture was blurred. He suddenly felt very uneasy.

"Gran, there are so many things I don't really know: one, what is a Srangle? Two," (and up came his second finger) "what does **Be, Mg, Ca, Sr, Ba, Ra** mean? and, three, why...?" but Sam stopped; and this time he did not hold up a finger. There were some whys he could never talk about.

His grandmother poured herself another cup of tea (she had six every morning without fail). His gran was just like toast, sharp and scratchy on the outside, soft and warm underneath.

"Perhaps Quwarndon, dear old Colonel Quwarndon would know? Call in on him on your way home from school. He was a scientist in the army. He knows lots of secret things. He'll know what **Bemg Casr Bara** means," (she said it like the title of an African chief) "and, certainly, what a Srangle looks like."

School was its usual boring self; but Toughie Wilson didn't try to beat him up, and Miss Austin forgot to be sarcastic about his spelling, so all in all it was quite a good day; except that he was going home to Dad's that night instead of to his grandmother's.

On Monday, Tuesday and Wednesday, he went to his gran's because his dad was working on those days. He worked for an airline and sometimes Sam didn't know exactly where his dad might be when it was bedtime.

The Colonel's house was not far from where he and his dad lived, so it was easy to make a detour to visit. As he opened the Colonel's front door, he felt his usual flash of delight.

From the outside, Colonel Quwarndon's house looked like an absolutely normal semi-detached, but inside he had removed all the inner walls and floors, and in the hollowed-out space he had built a large, shining aluminium rocket.

A gleaming oval, space-age rocket. Sam loved it.

"Hello, Colonel, it's me!" he called, grasping the rope ladder.

A short rope ladder labelled 'UP' led to the living capsule. Next to it, there was a metal pole arrowed 'DOWN'. So, though you had to climb up the swinging ladder, you could skim down the pole in no time at all. Then stairs went up again to the 'hot/wet' space (kitchen and bathroom to you and me), all in one area - shower opposite the stove, so the Colonel could keep an eye on the cooking while he was showering. He slept in the nose cone, which was a glass dome, poking out of the roof between the chimney and the TV aerial.

On Sam's birthday he had been invited to sleep there, while the Colonel hung in a bag in the living capsule.

"Hmm. Srangle, spangle, strangle, fangle, as in newfangled tangle, mangle, bangle, hmm. Now, let me see." The Colonel hovered in front of a wall of computers (really old-fashioned ones). "Yes, I knew I had heard of Srangles. I think, if I am not wrong, they are smallish, almost striped – no, maybe spotted, half a goat or half a dog, perhaps a touch of the ant eater; and you will find them in the White Forest. Yes, quite common down in the White Forest; you know, behind the Black Forest and to the west of the Green Forest. Make lovely pets. Was it the Lesser Spotted or the Greater Striped you were referring to?"

"I don't think it was striped or spotted," Sam said, trying desperately to recapture the details of his dream. The Colonel looked disappointed.

"Oh, the Common Srangle! Not anything like as interesting as the others, but…"

"Where is the White Forest, Colonel?" interrupted Sam hastily (the Colonel could go on a bit if left to his own devices). Right now, he was absent-mindedly glancing down at the strip of paper and running his fingers over the letters. Watching the Colonel standing there in his usual uniform of brown shorts, rugby shirt and sandalled feet, Sam was not totally convinced that the Colonel was as clever as his grandmother thought he was, but even so, he was still Sam's best friend.

"Oh, Sam, you are going to have to work out these letters by yourself. Yes, yes indeed! Well, well, what do they teach you at school? It's all community work, sex education and media studies no doubt, but right now I shall give your dad a buzz to ask if you can stay and have tea with me. Like that?"

Of course Sam did. While his dad always had plenty of food in the house, it was usually the sort of stuff that went straight from the freezer into the microwave. Now the Colonel – he was the most fantastic cook! The whole of one wall in the hot/wet space was given over to a deep freeze, fresh vegetable baskets and three ovens.

He was especially fond of tiny, dainty cakes, decorated with swirls of cream and crystallised fruits.

"I've tried kiwi-flavoured florentines today. Not at all sure they have worked. You can be the official taster."

Later, as Sam was about to shin down the pole

leading from the rocket to the front door, the Colonel said, "the third question, Sam? Your grandmother said you had three questions."

Sam looked at the Colonel's kindly, whiskery, clever old face and wanted so much to ask the third question, but he couldn't; he didn't have quite the right words in his mouth, so he just stared back at him.

"But remember, old chap. **Be**ryl the **M**a**g**nificent **ca**lled for **s**t**r**ong **ba**rgain **ra**dishes. Remember that, and you won't go far wrong."

St**r**ong **ba**rgain **ra**dishes? What's all this?

Sam walked home through the crowded streets, seeing nothing. His mind was so full of those dancing letters on stardust paper, **Be Mg Ca Sr Ba Ra**, and strange, difficult words. **Be**ryl the **M**a**g**nificent, **S**t**r**an-gles **ba**rking **ra**pidly, and **s**t**r**ong **ba**rgain **ra**dishes. Whatever could all that lot mean?

Chapter 2

Jelly the Sranglehund

Five days later, on opening the front door to his grandmother's flat, Sam found her standing there, umbrella in one hand and his roller blades in the other. Gran was round, smiley and dressed in floaty clothes covered in flower patterns.

"We have eight minutes before the bus passes along the main road, so boots on quickly." She was already wearing hers. She was the only grandmother Sam knew, who could manage an umbrella and a shopping bag at the same time as skimming along on roller blades, although she made a dreadful fuss going down the stairs in them.

They caught the bus and it was only then that Sam was able to ask,"What's the rush?"

"Well Sam, I have a feeling they close by 5.30."

"What closes?"

"The Dogs' Home."

He sat very still, just in case he had got it wrong.

Surely nobody went to a dogs' home unless they were looking for a dog. And if they were looking for a dog, that meant they wanted to keep a dog, in which case, they, that is, his grandmother and he would be taking a dog home with them.

Perhaps.

What about his dad? His dad liked everything clean and tidy and quiet and ordered. No dog would fit into that routine. And then, his gran lived in a flat. Problems.

To keep himself calm, he looked out of the window and concentrated on the names written over the shops, the street names and the signposts. The bus veered round to the left, down Black Forest Road.

BLACK FOREST!

What was it Colonel Quwarndon had said? 'Srangles could be found in the White Forest.' Was that next to the Black Forest? He couldn't remember.

White Forest! Sam glued his nose to the window, Stapleford Drive, Uppingham Street, Long Row, Winchester Close; street after street flew past. No White Forest or Green Forest.

"Sam, wake up, this is where we get off." His

eyes searched the buildings around him for street names, New Bridge Road? No. Butterton Terrace? No!

Oh well, it was only an idea.

The Dogs' Home was right down the end of the street and even before you got to it you could hear the howls, the barking and the yelps. They turned the corner and there in front of him, was a big arched gateway with huge wooden doors and a little door cut into one of them. Over the top was the sign.

"WHITE FOREST DOGS' HOME." Sam sighed happily – it was making a pattern.

The place was crammed full of dogs: big dogs, medium-sized dogs, tiny dogs, long-haired, short-haired, almost hairless, black, brown, white, spotted. It was overwhelming.

They walked in a confused daze as each dog in turn pleaded its case. 'Take me, take me, and take me,' they were saying with begging eyes, scrabbling feet and wagging tails. All except the mournful dogs; they had just given up in despair, or the angry ones, that snarled and growled in disgust at the whole process.

"Yes, we'll take that white Yorkshire Terrier; unless it's that big black Collie, or even the little curly-haired mongrel; or maybe… perhaps…" Grandmother was changing her mind every two minutes and Sam had long since given up.

Every one of them needed a home; how could he possibly choose just one?!

They had walked round the entire area twice peering into cages, when they suddenly found they had taken a wrong turning and had ended up in the cat and small animals' area. Cats and hamsters, rabbits, lizards and even snakes dozed contentedly. They were turning to go, when Sam caught sight of a strange animal.

Oh, it was a dog all right; big and orange and very hairy, but why was it with the cats? Gran and Sam stood staring at it curled up asleep on a pile of straw, when it slowly opened one eye, yawned, stretched, lifted its head and smiled at them. Yes, yes, it did; it gave a squinty, sideways grin, shambled to its feet, shook its great orange coat from side to side and ambled over to them.

"Ah, I see Jelly has taken a fancy to you." A voice like a foghorn boomed out behind them. They turned and there was one of the wardens. Sam could have sworn she was over six feet tall and almost as wide.

"We had to move her in here with the cats, because the noise out there was driving her wild. Very sensitive, this dog. Loves music, don't you Jelly? Schubert mostly."

"We'll take her." Sam said. Grandmother stared at him.

"This, little darling, this little Jelly-belly, needs at least thirty minutes exercise every morning and every evening, and your poor old grandmother doesn't look like she can totter down to the shops and back, let alone manage an hour's gallop across the park. So it will be up to you, lad." The Dogs' Home lady pinned him down with a fearsome glance and one extraordinarily big hand on his shoulder. Sam noticed his 'poor old grandmother,' who he knew was as tough as tractor tyres, was looking weak and droopy.

"Yes, of course I'll exercise her. And brush her, and feed her and all that stuff." Sam was almost whining.

" Right then, let's get the paper work done." She turned, ready to march them off to the office, when she suddenly stopped next to the rabbit cage.

"Come on Pretty-pink," she cooed," Treats for Pretty-pink." A tiny, fluffy, white rabbit hopped to the wire and the Dogs' Home lady, quickly stuffing her hand into her trouser pockets, dragged out a couple of radishes.

"Hungry, Pretty-pink?" she murmured as the rabbit delicately nibbled tiny bites out of the radishes that had been squeezed through the wire netting. " Get these cheap, from the man on the market." **Ba**rgain **Ra**dishes! Sam grinned with delight.

In the office it took ages to get the paper work finished, but at last they had signed all the bits of paper and Grandmother, Sam and Jelly were ready to leave.

"It's a bit of an odd-looking dog," Grandmother said as they turned to go.

" Oh yes, looks like half a dog and half a goat. It's

a hunting dog. Well, that's what the gentleman who brought it in told me. Came from Bavaria he did, and said he was dumping them because they were the most useless hunting dogs he had ever had. They call them Sranglehunds, out there in Bavaria, I believe. But he could have been making it all up, for all I know."

"You said 'them'?" Sam asked.

"Oh yes, he brought in a couple, Jelly and Custard. Little girl took Custard almost straight away. She wanted a dog that could run like the wind. Poor old Jelly moped no end after the other one went. Barked furiously all night. At one point we thought she'd die. The dog is really sensitive. If you have any trouble with her, come back and talk to me. " **Sr**angles **Bar**king **Ra**pidly! Or was it **Ba**rgain **Ra**dishes, it didn't matter he was living his dream, or had he dreamt his life?

"If anyone can keep an animal happy and healthy, Beryl, it's you," murmured his grandmother. Sam stared at the two of them. His grandmother knew this lady, this huge Beryl. Was she **Be**ryl the **Ma**gnificent? She certainly had something to do with **ra**dishes, and **Sr**angles. Secretly, Sam decided he would have called her Beryl the Beefy, rather than **Be**ryl the **Mag-**

nificent.

"I do my best, Letitia," murmured Beryl. Goodness! They did know each other, this Beryl and his grandmother; only her close friends called his grandmother, 'Letitia'. What was going on?

Chapter 3

The Fuchsia Pink Bike

"Gran, where's Green Forest?" Sam asked as they walked back to the bus stop.

"What?" replied Gran, about to answer when the bus pulled to a stop in front of them.

"Can we bring the dog on with us, please?" she was leaning forward, pleading with the driver.

"Dog! Do you call that a dog!" shouted the driver. "It's more like a goat, or a small camel! If my inspector knew I was letting half of London Zoo on board his buses, he would have my guts for garters. Why, I've seen cows smaller than that animal. You'll have to buy a ticket for it."

He suddenly stopped his tirade and smiled – Jelly was grinning her lop-sided soppy grin." Yeah, well, just this one time, call me soft, but it looks a friendly sort of animal and the bus isn't all that full."

The bus was full; it was almost packed solid, but nobody seemed to mind.

"Mrs. Marshall," murmured his grandmother as they settled down, "she said we could use her garden, now that her Poseypippens has died. That was a big dog as well, and I've already bought a kennel."

They had sat on the very back seat and Sam thought of dreams and **Sr**angles **ba**rking **ra**pidly and **Be**ryl the **M**a**g**nificent, and **st**r**o**ng **ra**dishes, and White and Black Forests. And those letters: **Be Mg Ca Sr Ba Ra.**

But most of all Sam thought about Jelly, leaning warm and solid against his legs. Little did he know that behind her loopy grin lay a mouth full of long, sharp, powerful teeth.

The next few days were wonderful. Jelly and Sam galloped through every park, every back street, every playground, and every canal path, riverside and wood. He got up early and stayed out late. Jelly never barked. She understood when and where it was OK to do dog poos. At night she slept under his bed and snored. Dog snores are quite quiet and gentle.

But then the day came when everything at school went wrong. Toughie Wilson had got his gang to help him with his bullying, throwing Sam's anorak into the puddle by the bike shed and then 'accidentally' stamping on it. Mrs Austin had nagged him incessantly about his spelling and his handwriting. Now here he was, sitting in the Head Mistress's office.

Mrs. Scratchily was beautiful on the outside, but she was really silly on the inside. Right now, she was fiddling with a pencil and speaking in that breathy little voice that she used when she wanted to be nice.

"Bones are funny things. Sometimes they are as strong as planks of wood and sometimes they are as soft as Edinburgh Rock. Do you know Edinburgh Rock?" Sam shook his head and watched the clock. For exactly four minutes Mrs. Scratchily waffled on, describing Edinburgh Rock.

"So you see Sam, breaking one of the small bones in your finger, isn't really all that much of a trouble. But now, old people, their bones are as fragile as Edinburgh Rock and sometimes they will break even a big bone."

Crack! She snapped the pencil between her fingers. Wow, that woman was made of steel. "And breaking a hipbone is really serious. For an old person like your grandmother, it can mean a stay in hospital for days, weeks, months..." she trailed off, and in the silence Sam suddenly understood what she was saying.

His grandmother was in hospital with a broken hipbone!

His days with his grandmother in her tiny cluttered flat were his lifeline. She had about six jigsaws on the go at any one time; they roller-bladed around the bus depot after dark; she got exciting DVDs from the shop. When he was at his father's, he read books, did his homework, and that was about it. What about Jelly? What would happen to Jelly?

He needed his grandmother!

"And I see from this schedule that your father is flying between Adelaide and Bahrain and will not be back for a fortnight at the least... So your Aunt Lucy has stepped into the breach."

Aunt Lucy? Sam hadn't got an Aunt Lucy.

"She will meet you from school. And she wants you to remember that her new bike is pink, not purple, like the last one. Pink. OK?"

At home-time Sam sneaked out of school, head down. He was looking for some batty old woman with a pale pink bike.

There was the usual scrum of cars, pushchairs, mothers and children, as thick as lemon curd around the gate: the mothers nattering, the kids running, the babies screaming. It was chaos. At the end of the street there was a crow's nest of the older boys. Sam tried to squeeze past. How was he going to recognize this Aunt Lucy?

"Wow, look at that Harley," muttered a senior boy.

"Is that a Harley–Davidson?" squeaked a much smaller one.

There was a sort of hush hanging over the group, and in the middle, poised on tiptoe was a fantastic motorbike. It was more like a space age dragon than a bike; all gleaming curved metal sides, and interlocking machinery. It was painted an iridescent, brilliant, fuchsia pink. The rider standing next to it was wearing pink leathers.

It was a woman. A small, dainty lady with bubbling yellow curls.

"Hi Sam! Here's your helmet." The pink-leathered lady held a black helmet towards him, "Get on – we'll pop straight down to the hospital."

Stepping forward towards the bike as the circle of senior boys fell back a little, Sam could hear what sounded like a group sigh. He had never, ever, been on a motorbike, and he had no idea how to get on. But now was not the time to mention it. So, grasping that bit at the top of the bike, and leaping kangeroo-high, he jumped and somehow, landed on the pillion seat.

"Well, yes! Either a ballet dancer, or a pole-vaulter in waiting," murmured the pink lady. And with that, the whole monster growled into life and purred off down the street.

Never had Sam felt anything so fantastic. It was just one notch below sky-diving. It was much better

than flying. They dipped and swerved in and out of the half-stationary, rush hour traffic. Lorry drivers flashed their lights at them as they streamed past, and on small sections of the road without speed restrictions, the whole machine leapt forward, more like a dolphin than a bike. Clutching onto the waist of this strange Aunt Lucy, Sam grinned from ear to ear, half frightened, half so happy, he wanted to whoop with delight.

All too quickly the flying, swooping, diving ride ended, and there they were at the hospital.

His poor grandmother was looking very small and very crumpled, with purple bruises everywhere. Colonel Quwarndon was looking worried. The hospital was white and shiny, a bit like the Colonel's space rocket, and the air hummed.

"I haven't actually told them how I managed to fall so badly," grandmother was whispering, "but it was when my umbrella got hooked on a railing while I was roller-blading home with a very heavy bag of dog food on my other arm, so I'm bashed on one side and crushed on the other." She looked dreadful. "And maybe my wrist is just a little bit broken."

"Listen," interrupted Lucy, in a quiet, smiling sort of voice, not at all like his gran's matter-of-fact tones, or the Colonel's firm military way, "don't worry about Sam or Jelly. Sam can have my spare room and Jelly will have the back garden." She nibbled a few grapes.

"Yes," added the Colonel, "he can have tea with me on the afternoons Lucy is working, and remember I have a huge garden; we could make a run for Jelly."

"Right, that's organised," smiled Aunt Lucy, nail-polished finger about to take the last of the grapes, "Well, that is, until I have to go to the Utah."

His grandmother and Colonel Quwarndon, both swivelled their heads round to look at her.

"Oh, No!" moaned his grandmother, "The Daring Devils race across the flats of Utah; your biggest event of the year."

Colonel Quwarndon turned to Sam, "Lucy is a motorbike journalist, she writes articles for newspapers about bikes, and she comments on radio or TV when there's a race. And sometimes she rides in a race."

Rides in motorcycle races! Sam gazed at this tiny,

pink and pretty aunt he had just been given.

There was a long silence, and finally his grandmother straightened her back and declared in a bossy sort of voice: "Well, I shall be better by then! Won't I?"

While it was indeed a rough time for his grandmother, Aunt Lucy turned out to be the most astonishing of aunts.

She lived in what was, possibly, the most neglected of houses, and produced the most unimaginative food Sam had ever experienced but she lived a wonderful life.

"Come on, Sam, gobble up those beans, it's tenpin bowling tonight." Aunt Lucy's cooking did not stretch beyond beans on toast, eggs on toast and cheese on toast. But her evening activities were so exciting: bowling or skating, rock wall climbing or kayaking. But she always insisted that first of all he walked Jelly, and then they visited his frighteningly frail grandmother.

With all the excitement of moving to Lucy's, looking after Jelly and worrying about his grandmother, he had almost forgotten about the scrap of paper with its strange letters. Almost, but not quite.

Aunt Lucy was a good listener, and Sam found he was telling her things he had never mentioned to either his father or grandmother.

"Toughie Wilson… well he is much bigger than me… and he doesn't have red hair does he? So…'

'Yes, but does that give him the right to bully you! No sir! I think tomorrow we will use the Kawasaki. That bike is a big, loud animal."

In Aunt Lucy's securely locked and bolted garage she had the gleaming pink Harley Davidson, the mid-night blue Kawasaki, and the fantastic scarlet Ducati. Three mouth-wateringly gorgeous motorbikes!

Next door lived Ken, who drove a battered van for distributing sacks of potatoes, and one evening Lucy had said, "Of course I never use the bikes as a get-away vehicle. Ken lends me his van for that." Sam had pondered a long time about that 'get-away' sen-tence. It sounded like the sort of thing bank robbers said. So why did Aunt Lucy need a 'get-away vehicle'?

Not that she was a real aunt. It seemed that Lucy's mother had been frequently ill when Lucy was a baby, and so his grandmother had often stepped in to look after the baby Lucy. Later her whole family had moved away, and it was only in the last few months that Lucy, on her own, had returned to the area and again met up with his grandmother.

The next morning the little posse of senior boys who had started to hang around the school gates, just on the off chance of catching a glimpse of one of the bikes, was rewarded by the flash and roar of the shimmering, midnight-blue Kawasaki, with both riders black from head to toe, except for a jagged silver streak down each arm (Lucy's old leathers fitted Sam really well).

It had felt to Sam, as they powered through the streets, that they were riding a massive, fire-breathing dragon or a war horse and that he and Lucy were knights in armour, ready for battle.

"Carry your bag, Sam," pleaded Toughie Wilson. Wriggling out of the black leathers, Sam murmured, "Fine – think the bike might need the preload damping adjusted."

He hadn't the faintest idea what that sentence meant but, oh! It sounded good. Life was sweet. But it was not to last.

Chapter 4

The Letters Return

"So, is that decided then? I buy the food," declared the Colonel, " Letitia, you cook it, and Sam you do the housework. OK?" There was a serious moment of silence, "And then, next week your dad will be back for a month, so you, Sam, can go home, and you, Letitia, you can build up your strength." They were all gathered round his grandmother as she sat propped up in the hospital bed. The very next day, Aunt Lucy was leaving for her trip to Utah.

For one long moment, Sam had wanted to say that home was with his grandmother; that what he wanted was to have Jelly, the Colonel, Lucy and his grandmother as his family, but he knew you cannot just choose your family. After all, he was only a skinny red-haired boy who was a bit of a nuisance to all these kind, hard-working adults who were doing their best for him. And at that moment, he didn't feel he could tell them about the knife that Spike Simms, Toughie

Wilson's shadow, kept in his trouser pocket.

"Better take Jelly out first of all, and then the bathroom needs a good clean." Gran, now home, was peeling potatoes, standing at the work surface, barricaded in by chairs so that she could not topple over.

Sam was so pleased that his grandmother's steak and kidney puddings and chicken casseroles had replaced the beans and toast offered by Lucy, but he was worried about the way she had become so much smaller and more frail-looking. Much as he had enjoyed himself with Aunt Lucy, it was wonderful to have Gran home again, almost mended.

"There's an awful lot of this cleaning stuff, isn't there?" He had washed and dusted, polished and scrubbed for the past two weeks.

"You are a star, Sam. The house is beautiful." She turned slowly, her old bones clicking, and looked at him very carefully, "Well, what is it? Tell me." She could usually tell when he was excited about something.

"I came home through the wood… and..." he said slowly and paused. He had escaped to his special wood, where he could forget all the horrible things that had happened to him that day at school. He wasn't going to tell Gran that now he was no longer roaring to school on the back of a high-powered motor bike, Toughie Wilson had started bullying all over again. Nor was he going to tell her how Spike Simms would slip a long, shining blade in and out of his pocket every time he jostled Sam in passing. It was bad enough to have to acknowledge that no matter how hard he tried, he still got words muddled up and Miss Austin seemed to delight in sniffing loudly when she marked his work. "… and… I was right in the middle of the wood when I found another one."

Another fragment of shining paper. He had pounced on it. This time the hexagons were tinted gold, glinting, more like powdered flakes of sun than floating stardust. Was it the shimmering, flickering beauty of the paper that excited him or was it the tiny hope that perhaps the letters would grow into a new dream? There were only four letters this time.

"Let's see!" She said holding out a dripping wet hand, " Oh, yes." They both stared down at the letters,

H Li Na K

"Those letters don't make a word do they? Could that be somebody's name?" They both stood silent, puzzling over the strange combination of letters.

"Perhaps your dad will be able to work them out. He's a clever man, and he's home tomorrow. Only one more night here with me and then you'll be back with your dad for a bit," she smiled at him and Sam loved her soft wrinkly face. "Now I have some lovely music for you to listen to tonight: Grieg's 'In the hall of the Mountain King'. But you had better be off with that Sranglehund dog before it gets dark."

It was raining, a fine, dull, grey rain, and this time the two of them ran to the park, sprinted around the football pitches, scuttled under and around the empty swings, dashed from one corner to the other and then home again. It was strange in the empty park, now that the misty light filled the corners with shifting mauve shadows, but Sam didn't stop to look; he just wanted to make himself tired. He wanted to be so tired that he could dream of flying up through his star-painted ceiling into another world.

"Here you are, Sam, try listening to this in bed

tonight," said his grandmother when they'd eaten the rabbit stew and raspberry crumble and Sam had washed the dishes.

Tucked up in his tiny bedroom Sam took out the shiny scrap of paper;

H Li Na K

Perhaps a foreign language, like Lithuanian or Serbo-Croat? The last time he had found the shining paper with its special letters he had dreamt of barking Srangles. Maybe tonight he would dream of **h**yenas and **li**ons **na**tive to **K**enya. Or **h**eavenly **li**quorices **nas**tily **k**idnapped. His hand found the painted treasure box squeezed tightly next to the wall behind his bed; now there would be two bits of shiny paper folded up inside. And underneath them his other treasures, the cards, all fourteen of them, but only two in envelopes. He took the cards out most evenings, just to touch, sometimes to smell.

Sam switched on the disc player and gazed up at his starry sky. Sleep, soft and warm like porridge, seeped around him and he fell almost immediately to sleep. He always tried so hard to dream of flying, but he never did and tonight was no different. But he did dream.

Such a weird dream full of the tall, stiff letters, **H Li Na K**, which kept tripping him up, and hurling him over. Or was it he, himself, who was flinging things about? Perhaps his dream was really all about Toughie Wilson and Spike Simms?

Toughie was not in school the next day and so Sam just floated through the lessons, until the end-of-school bell brought him down to earth with a bump.

He had walked home very, very slowly; he didn't want to go home. It was not that his dad was unkind or cruel; it was that living with him was so … so… well…so boring – everything just so, all put away, all neat, all tidy, all very, very quiet.

"Hi son!" called out his dad as he opened the door to the flat.

"Hi, Dad." He stood, uncertain what to say. It had been such a busy time since his father went away and he wasn't sure if his father knew all the twists and turns of the story. Should he tell him about Jelly, or the letters, or his funny dreams or even about Toughie Wilson? Did he actually know that he had been staying with Aunt Lucy and riding about town on her bike?

"Well, that was a bit of high drama wasn't it? But you lot seem to have managed perfectly well without me. I know your grandmother is quite old, but somehow I'd never really stopped to think what would happen if she broke a bone or two. Anyhow, we have been hatching a plan. Come on. Why are you hovering in the hall?"

In the lounge sat Gran, Colonel Quwarndon, Aunt Lucy (back from Utah) and of all people, Beryl the Magnificent, the lady from the Dogs' Home. There were cups and plates and glasses everywhere. In fact the place looked quite a mess. Sam just stared.

"I didn't know you knew each other," he blurted out.

"Oh, it's my fault, old boy," interjected the Colonel. "I know Lucy because I know your Grandmother. Beryl and I, we get organic veg from the same farmers' market. And remember, I was a science teacher, and your Dad was my star pupil, before we both met up again in the army." Sam had thought that the Colonel was his grandmother's friend, not his dad's.

"Actually it was the Colonel who made a wonderful suggestion which just about saved my sanity when I was around your age," said Dad quietly.

There was a sudden hush in the room – everybody was looking at his dad, who was looking down at his hands, and Sam noticed his white knuckles, showing how tightly those hands were gripped together.

"So," boomed Beryl, "this is where I come in – now my brother is the best karate teacher in this town; indeed in this county. 'Natural Karate' he teaches – you have to follow the laws of nature, the natural cycle of the year."

"Yes?" said Sam. He had no idea why she was telling him all of this.

"We all thought that if you had one or two finely-tuned, beautifully executed karate throws up your sleeve, perhaps the Toughie Wilsons of this world would think twice about slinging your school bag across the road." It was Aunt Lucy who said that.

How did they know about that? He had told nobody about yesterday's incident.

Karate? Wouldn't all the rest of the class laugh at him. It could be another place where he would make a fool of himself.

"I thought," said Aunt Lucy quietly, " as you'd shown so much ability when we went skating, and canoeing, that you'll be good at karate as well."

"And," went on his grandmother, "when you are out and about with Jelly, I want to be sure you are able to look after yourself."

"Which is just what the Colonel suggested for me, all those years ago, when I was being bullied," said his dad. Sam stared at his tall, handsome father. Who would bully him?

"Why, I mean, why did they pick on you?"

"Oh, it was just that I was clever – they hate anyone who is different."

" I had a rough time as well," bellowed Beryl. "It was because I was so big, they hate big kids. And my brother Lindly – they picked on him because he was so tall, thin and lanky. Lanky Lindly, they called him."

“Were you bullied as well, Gran?” asked Sam. His grandmother shook her head:

“No, I was small but a bit fiery.”

They all turned to look at Lucy, who suddenly blushed. ” Well, to be honest, and I am not proud of it, but I was a bit of a bully at times.”

Sam gasped and to his surprise suddenly felt so much better; bullied, bullying, it was something everyone had to learn to cope with. All these grown-ups; they knew about bullying; it was not something that had happened only to him.

"OK," he agreed, quietly," I think this karate idea is great.” And turning to Beryl, ” is he still called Lanky Lindly?“

Chapter 5

Mugged

Beryl walked with him round to the gym where her brother worked. He was about six foot six tall and every one called him 'Hi Lindly'. Sam could join the classes and was to start the very next evening.

It was only when Sam was lying in his large, cool, pale bedroom: white floor, white walls and cream curtains that he remembered his dream of the night before; all the throwing and the falling, and he thought of his new letters:

H Li Na K

Did they mean '**Hi Lin**dly's **Na**tural **K**arate' ?

What strange patterns there were in life, he mused, as he drifted off to sleep. Perhaps **Hi Lin**dly really would teach him **Na**tural **K**arate so he could defend himself, and perhaps one day he would be able to throw Toughie Wilson and his school bag half way across the street, and then he'd trip up Spike Simms and grab his knife. And what about his spelling, would

Natural Karate help with that as well?

Karate was held every evening in the big ugly gym hall, just three streets away. It was a very successful enterprise with children jostling in and out all evening.

Lining up with all the other boys, waiting for the earlier class to finish, Sam's heart missed a beat. There, in the midst doing some very impressive throws, was Toughie Wilson himself. To get back to the changing room, Toughie would come right past the place where Sam was standing. He glanced over his shoulder, no escape route that way; at least seven other children were wedged in behind him, another four in front. He was stuck.

The class finished with some crisp, quick, strange foreign words and the older boys were striding down towards the door.

"Well, if it isn't bird's nest after all," jeered Toughie. Sam ran a nervous hand over his unruly mop of red frizz.

"Yes and didn't you know curls always cover brains and fire- sharp reflexes, while a plain old mousy wig like yours is a disguise for nothing – just a small empty hole."

The voice spat out the words level with his shoulder and peering round Sam saw furious brown eyes, a golden brown face and a huge mane of tight black curls. The boys behind Toughie laughed.

"Watch out mate, that one can bite. Go on Spitfire, teach him a lesson." The girl just tossed her head.

"If you had something other than straw on your head you wouldn't have the brains of a scarecrow," she continued…

"OK. We get it," mumbled Toughie, as she strode past them, straight and strong.

"Right, guys," said the immensely tall skinny instructor, Hi Lindly or Hi Lo as Sam soon learnt to call him. "We have a new lad with us today, show him all the respect we give everyone, and Spitfire you look after him. Sam you shadow her. She's ace." The girl danced across the room to his side; she radiated self-confidence. " Sam, we all have new names in this class, so I'm calling you Firefly. You look small and sharp and hot as lightning."

Firefly! Small and sharp and hot as lightning! Wow!

The next hour flew past. The moves! The application! Nobody talked, everybody concentrated; by eight that evening Sam was dripping sweat, exhausted and supremely happy, and the rest of the week wasn't so bad after all. The quiet gentle calm of the flat after the hustle and bustle of school was really rather nice.

On Mondays Lucy took him ice-skating and on Thursdays there was karate where he tried extremely hard to learn everything as quickly as possible. Spitfire took her duties as his monitor very seriously so that he was being coached not only by Hi Lo but also by the fiery, dancing, Spitfire. On Saturday he, his dad and Colonel Quwardon took Gran, still shaky on her slowly-healing hip, out for the day.

"Anywhere, anywhere my dears, just as long as all I will need is one hip. Why were we not given four legs? Then we could lose one and still be mobile."

"You can ride a bike with one leg," suggested the Colonel, sweetly. Gran scowled at him. She wanted two good strong legs, not one wobbly bike.

Life was great, but then it happened. On his way home from school one Friday, he became aware that there was a group of boys following him.

As he crossed the road, so would they; when he turned down a side street, so would they. He was half way down a little narrow alleyway when he realized that one of them was Toughie Wilson, the other, Spike Simms and the third, Jaz, who never said anything, but giggled at whatever Toughie did.

It was too late to turn back on to the main road. Blindly, he swerved down a side street he had not noticed before. It was a bad decision. The street was a dead end, just a short cul-de-sac, with no exit at the far end. On either side there were terraced houses without front gardens. At the far end there was a high brick wall, with boarded-up houses on each side.

Reaching the wall, Sam turned in panic.

The three boys were now spread out across the street, walking silently towards him, grinning. He couldn't remember a thing he had learnt in karate. All his muscles turned hard and tight, so that he could not move. His throat was so tight, he wouldn't be able to shout for help.

He was powerless and Toughie and his mates still kept coming, slowly now, playing cat and mouse. Toughie was whistling tunelessly between his teeth.

The road was very quiet, even the houses were waiting.

Think, Sam, think, he told himself, and suddenly he remembered what Hi Lo had said last week, 'Turn sideways, plant your legs firmly on the ground and breathe deep and slow.' He had just managed to do that and no more when the first blow landed on his shoulder.

"Come on Firefly, let's see you fly!" jeered Toughie; lashing out at him a blow so hard, it jolted all the breath from his body. Seconds later, air rushed into his lungs and, suddenly, he found that he was yelling at the top of his voice. He meant to shout ' HELP!' but it came out as a desperate, frantic howl instead. At the same time he started to spin, duck and weave, dodging the blows that were landing on his back, his face, and his stomach. Now he was screaming and shouting, half in fear and half in desperation.

"Fly, fly, fly!" chanted the gang as they rained slaps and punches down on him. He was scared. Scared he was going to fall down. Scared they would kick him. Scared he'd cry. Scared Spike would pull out his knife. Scared they'd kill him! All he could do was to try and keep upright, to keep on his feet. By twisting and dodging, he tried to find a gap between them, so he could make a dash for it and run off down the street.

It was then that he saw the dogs. There were two of them galloping down the street towards him. It was Jelly and another almost identical to her, both with their lips pulled right back in great toothy snarls. Seconds later the two, big, powerfully angry dogs were upon them. With a yelp and roar they leapt onto the boys, bowling two of them to the ground with a single blow. Jaz spun round, saw what had happened and ran away as fast as he could, screaming with fear as he ran. Sam, battered and breathless, turned and staggered over towards the other two, still cringing on the ground below the snarling, growling, dripping, open mouths of the dogs.

"Here Jelly," he gasped…"Here…" Could this other dog actually be Custard, the other Sranglehund who had been in the Dogs' Home with Jelly? "Here Custard." Both dogs ambled over and sat quietly at his heels. Toughie and Spike scrambled to their feet and tore off down the street without a backward glance.

Sam, knelt on the ground with his arms round each dog, shivering with pain and relief. "Oh Jelly, my wonderful, marvellous, fantastic dog." When he finally managed to clamber to his feet he felt for the new dog's collar.

It had a brown leather collar with a small dangling metal disc: 'Custard' it said, with a telephone number.

Chapter 6

Custard

Stumbling home, Sam collapsed against the front door and his horrified dad dragged him in, allowing both dogs in as well – something he had never done before.

"Sam, what happened? Oh! Good God, look at you! Let's get your grandmother."

His grandmother arrived with creams, lotions, pills, cold compresses, warm compresses, chicken soup and ice cream.

Later, much later, when Sam was patched up, fed the chicken soup and tucked up in bed his dad came back into the room. "Well, according to Mrs. Wilson, Toughie and his two friends were picked up in her Range Rover two minutes after school finished and all three were playing upstairs on the computer from that moment on until the time when the police arrived, and she says you must have made a mistake. According to the police it's your word against theirs, as no one else witnessed the attack." He sat down on the end of the bed and sighed.

"I thought they'd say that, Dad. They'd never admit to being beaten by a midget like me, and two dogs." At this, his dad grinned for the first time that evening.

"What about Custard?"

"Oh, I rang the number on the dog's collar, got an address and the taxi that brought your grandmother round agreed to take the dog back, so I slipped a twenty pound note into an envelope and tied it to his collar."

"Thanks Dad."

"By the way, you have a visitor."

Colonel Quwarndon shuffled into the room. He was wearing his usual khaki shorts, purple striped pullover and sandals and, for some strange reason, gloves. He was trying to look sympathetic but actually looked extremely pleased with himself. A small tangle of wires and gadgets dangled from one hand and Sam's anorak was stuffed under the other arm.

"Only a camera at the moment; you have it in your pocket, while this fibre optic goes into this little lens, buried here in the pin which I will attach to the front of your anorak. Normally the whole apparatus is switched off, but in an emergency, you squeeze this button and all is operational. So you film the whole incident. It is a cinecamera."

"Wow, it's worth being mugged to have stuff like that in my pocket."

"I knew this little gadget would come in handy when I …er…left...left…" he trailed off.

"You stole that from the army?"

"Not entirely, it was my invention in the first place; this was the prototype so it was mine in spirit. It has night vision, of course, as well. Do you like the pin?" The pin attached to the front of the jacket was a small round red firefly; the lens, disguised as a round, shiny jewel, making up its many-angled eye.

"It's great, Colonel, I'm really looking forward to my next mugging." The Colonel giggled.

"How did Jelly get to me?" Sam asked.

"Oh, yes, very strange. She set up the most dreadful howling. I ran down, thinking she had caught herself in the wire fencing. When I opened the gate, she practically jumped over me, howling all the time, and galloped off down the street, and I was convinced

I could hear a barking from over the other side of the canal as well."

Sam thought for a moment, "Did she hear me shouting? When she started to howl, Custard could've heard her howl and recognised it as Jelly's bark and set up barking in response – then he managed to get out and the pair of them tracked down my cries. I was yelling a lot. Yes, I was yelling all the time."

Sam lay back, he was bruised and battered all over, and his head throbbed, but his grandmother and father were in the living room talking, the Colonel was sitting quietly beside him and Jelly lay under the bed; and maybe tomorrow he would find another scrap of paper.

Of course, Toughie, Spike and Jaz were still there, at school, but with the new camera deep in his pocket, its lens peeping out of the badge pinned to his jacket, walking to and from school wasn't too bad. He photographed every thing just by pressing a button in his pocket, then, in the evening he deleted everything so he could start afresh the next day. Walking home was especially frightening but he now kept to the main roads and had the camera switched on all the time. He wore the camera when he took Jelly out, before and after school. It gave him confidence to wander much further field.

"All this exercise is making you grow. You're not such a little weed any more," said his grandmother - she could be so tactless at times. But still, he was glad he was growing. Perhaps his hair would calm down as he grew bigger. Perhaps he would learn to spell. Then he'd be big and tall and strong, with sensible smooth hair and his father would think he was wonderful and he would be able to really help his grandmother and he would ask them both that question which worried him so much.

Then one afternoon when he was exploring a new canal path, an extraordinary thing happened. Jelly, who was normally the most steady and reliable of dogs, suddenly leapt forward yanking, her lead out of Sam's hand as she streaked away down the path.

"Jelly, Jelly! Come back!" he yelled.

Jelly ignored him.

Then Sam saw why: galloping towards them

down the other side of the canal was an identical dog – long floppy ears, long gangling legs, and orange fur flying. And behind, shouting as loud as he was, came a girl.

"Custard, you stupid mutt! Come here!" Even from that distance, Sam could see her mop of curly black hair.

It was Spitfire! Spitfire from karate.

The two dogs stopped, each on their own side of the canal, and barked uproariously. Sam and Spitfire stood on their own sides shouting at each other.

Suddenly ears flying, fur flapping, Jelly took an almighty leap forward and landed with a resounding splash in the middle of the canal.

Sam froze. Spitfire gasped and Jelly, heavy with wet fur, sank below the surface of the stinking black water, rose to the surface, and sank again. Silence. She was gone. The black-green water closed thick and smooth over her head.

Sam felt a fear as he had never, ever felt it before. He should jump in and try to save her but he was paralysingly afraid of the black water, the straight vertical green slippery sides of the canal itself and the thick mud at the bottom.

Seconds later, the dog's head bobbed up again and this time she started to thrash around, paddling noisily in great circles in the middle of the canal. Custard was howling furiously all the time. Slowly, splashing and spluttering, Jelly started to swim towards the other bank. By now, Spitfire was lying on her stomach, arms outstretched over the water and then, at last...

"I've got her, Sam, got her collar. Come on old dear. Up you come," and struggling and heaving, she dragged the great wet, but suddenly thin dog out of the water. Jelly clambered to her feet and shook, sending an arching shower of stinking canal water flying all over the still-seated Spitfire.

"Oi! less of that, I've just saved your life, no need to drown me." At this point Sam was laughing and jumping and shouting, and the two dogs were capering round and round each other in excited little circles.

"Where's the nearest bridge, so I can cross over?" he called.

"Oh, miles down the path, you'll have to..." but Sam had already set off running.

"I had no idea Custard belonged to you," he gasped as he padded up to them. "It was Custard who helped me escape when I was being beaten up."

"I had no idea that it was you who got Jelly from the Dogs' Home, and I had no idea it was your dad who sent Custard back to us in the taxi, after he ran away, " she replied, still sitting on the grass, her arms wrapped round the squirming Custard.

"I think they must be brother and sister, from the same litter. Look at them! They are so happy to be together. It's a bit weird, us knowing each other, and them knowing each other, but neither of us knowing that we even had a dog, let alone two dogs related to each other." Sam rubbed his head. Suddenly noticing how wet Spitfire was, "How far are you from home? I suppose I ought to get Jelly back so I can dry her."

"Oh, it's only a couple of streets away," replied Spitfire clambering up onto her feet. "Shall we meet up here tomorrow and take the dogs out together?" Spitfire, always confident, saying the one thing Sam would never have dared to suggest.

"Great." he agreed, happily. "See you tomorrow. Come on, you great wet lollipop – let's get you home."

For both Sam and Spitfire it was so good to have someone else to share their walks and (while he'd never told Spitfire about the scraps of shining paper he had found) Sam had finally introduced her to his special wood.

One afternoon they decided to play hide and seek while they were there.

"You and Custard hide; Jelly and I will wait two minutes, then I say to Jelly 'Find Custard. Find' and we see how long it takes her to find you." Sam suggested.

"Great," said Spitfire, "come on Custard. Come on! Just drop that, it's only a scrap of paper." She bent down, fishing something out of Custard's mouth. "Oh look Sam, it's rather pretty." She held out a square of paper decorated with shining, shimmering hexagons. It was his stardust paper.

Snatching it before she managed to turn it over and catch sight of the letters, Sam muttered "You go and hide – I'll let you have this after we've played the game," quickly stuffing the paper into his pocket.

Another set of letters, another shining scrap of paper, another adventure and another surprise! His letters, his dreams, his surprises.

He liked Spitfire; it was fun to be with her but this was his secret. He had only told his grandmother and the Colonel about the paper and the letters because he needed their help. She was not part of his mystery. He was not going to let her see the letters. He was not going to tell her anything.

They played until it was getting dark, the dogs getting quicker and quicker each time, until Spitfire said, "I've got to rush. It will be dark in a few minutes. See you tomorrow," and she was gone.

With the shiny paper and its strange letters still in his pocket, he ran back to the Colonel's. He shoved Jelly into her kennel and clambered up the ladder into the Colonel's rocket-shaped home.

"Colonel, look, look another one! Look!" The pattern was different, more like interlocking stars, but the paper was just as enchanting, made of colours where moonlight and sunshine mingled. And of course, different letters.

B C N O F

Chapter 7

B C N O F

The Colonel wiped his hands on his apron, took the paper carefully and smoothed it with his thumb. "Making chocolate coated meringues with crystallised ginger cream," he said by way of explanation. "Let's see what we have here. **B C N O F**" he murmured slowly. "They seem very familiar. Have you looked the sequence up on the internet?"

"Not yet." said Sam, eyeing the cakes. They looked incredible; tiny mountains, crisp and white with a deep chocolate base. "Bits of crystallised ginger?" he asked.

The Colonel put the paper down and broke a meringue in half, "Yes. Just perfect! Shall we have a nibble before we get down to serious thinking?" And it was only long afterwards that Sam realised they had never got down to serious thinking, and that the last thing the Colonel had said as he waved goodbye was, "Oh, yes! Your grandmother left this CD for your music tonight; seems it's Muddy Waters singing 'Walking thru' the Park'."

School had been OK that day – not brilliant, but reasonably OK. Toughie Wilson and his gang had glared at him but that was all. Still, just to make sure he was safe, Sam checked and rechecked that his camera was there – tucked in safely, but discreetly hidden in his pocket.

In the end it hadn't mattered because Aunt Lucy had roared up to the school gate on her red Ducati and had whisked him straight round to the Colonel's. As he and Lucy careered along the side streets, he'd noticed Toughie and his lot lounging about at the end of the road where he had had his horrible encounter with them. He wondered (with an icicle of fear) if they were planning another attempt at beating him up.

Leaving Aunt Lucy and the Colonel eating their second round of bilberry-banana muffins, he'd unlocked the gate to Jelly's enclosure when he had a sudden and quite surprising flashback. He remembered the dream he'd had the night before – but only bits of it. It was something to do with the canal where Jelly had taken her unexpected swim, he was sure of that. But why did he think it was the canal? It had been such a strange dream, in which he had been trying to find his way to a party, and then there had been something else … what was it? What was it? And how did the canal fit in? Somehow he had got from the party to the canal. The half-remembered bits niggled at his mind. It was important; he knew it was important.

At the end of the street, Spitfire was waiting for him, with Custard quietly asleep at her feet. "Lets walk right along the canal as far as we can," she said as soon as he was close enough to hear. His dream was about the back of the canal.

"We want to go to the back of the canal…" he replied and Spitfire butted in:

"Next to the open field."

That was it! That was what he had dreamt. He had woken up with those actual words on his mind:

'Back of the canal next to the open field.'

"How did you know that?" he demanded, half cross and half amazed. "How did you know – back of the canal next to the open field?"

Spitfire stopped walking and stared at him, then

said slowly, "We went there, you and I, 'back of the canal next to an open field'. I mean in my dream last night we did. I'm not sure why, because my dream was all about me going to a dance class in a hall at the back of the canal. I had to wear this stupid yellow costume, but then I woke up this morning and just sat up and said it. I said those words, *'back of the canal next to an open field.'* "

"Well, I don't understand any of this but that's exactly…I mean *exactly*, what I dreamt last night."

"You were wearing a stupid yellow costume for a dance class? Oh lovely!" hooted Spitfire.

"No way! No; my dream was all about going to a party, but somehow or other I woke up thinking that I had to go to that open field at the back of the canal." And then Sam remembered the letters he'd found '**B C N O F**'. Letters, which had turned themselves into these whole words, **b**ack of a **c**anal **n**ext to an **o**pen field. The letters he had prevented Spitfire from seeing.

"Ohhh? Am I picking up your dreams or are you blundering into mine?" she was laughing.

"That's ridiculous!" said Sam. "It's probably

something we were talking about yesterday and it sort of got stuck in our brains and you let it slip into your dream and I did the same thing." He said it firmly but he was not at all sure if that was the truth.

They were now marching briskly along the canal path, both silent. Suddenly Spitfire ran forward shouting, "Look Sam, look at the pub sign!" In front of them was a crumbling old pub, and hanging from a hook on the side of the building was a wooden board with the name of the pub painted on it.

"CANAL BACK" Sam yelled. "Is there an open field next to it?"

Spitfire was ahead, running like a cheetah. They careered round to the front. A road - shops down one side and there, opposite a small paddock.

"Back of the canal next to an open field," breathed Spit-

fire. "There's our field! Now what? What do we do now Sam?" They walked up to the paddock.

"What's so special about this? It's a tatty old field; just scrappy rough grass, with that mucky path going up to the hedge," said Sam.

The pair of them leant against the gate, gazing around with a sense of deep disappointment. Behind them was the pub, a large billboard advertising the performance of the Moldavian Ballet Company, and a newspaper shop. In front was the dreary little field, with a path leading diagonally up a slight slope to the hedge at the top. Behind the hedge was a hill covered in trees and behind that, Sam could see the faint outlines of a huge house. Neither of them said anything.

With her nail file Spitfire scratched into the wood of the gate: 'Back Canal Next Open Field' underlining the capitals **B C N O F**. They were the letters he had kept secret from her. Suddenly she turned to him and said "Toughie Wilson lives in that house."

"Which house?"

"That huge, grand, palatial mansion up there behind the wood."

"Are you sure?"

"Yes, my mum used to go up there cleaning. That was before the Wilson's bought it last year," and then she added (perhaps the worst words he had ever heard), "Toughie Wilson dreamt about this canal as well."

"What do you mean?"

"Well, I didn't tell you this before, but this afternoon I'd rushed out of school really quickly so that I could walk home with you, because I'd sort of discovered that Toughie Wilson was up to something."

"Like what?" asked Sam, suddenly anxious.

"Well, you know he's in my class? He'd chucked a note at that stupid Jaz. You know, his pet gorilla? Jaz had read it, smirked, and then torn it in two, screwed up the bits and slung them in the bin."

"Yes?"

"So, at playtime I rescued it, but I only got one bit. " She passed across a slip of torn crumpled paper:

GET OUR OWN BAC
RED SHRIMP
AMBUSH
SCOOL

"Doesn't school have an 'h' in it? And what does 'red shrimp' mean?"

Spitfire looked at him and sort of shrugged. "You are a bit short, aren't you? And, I mean, you do have reddish hair. So I thought the whole thing probably said something like..."

Sam completed her sentence, "Something like: 'Get our own back on that red shrimp, and ambush him after school' Yes? And I suppose I'm the Red Shrimp?"

"Now, listen this is absolutely weird. I wanted to find out what they were really up to so I stalked them all day. They were just coming out of the boys' toilets when I heard Toughie say something like this… wait a minute… let me get it right, he said 'Had a brill dream last night, I was in this boxing ring, *back of the canal next to the open field* and I was just knocking everyone out, bam, wham, just like that.' "

How were all of them, he himself, Spitfire and Toughie, all of them dreaming the same dream? It was his dream! They were his letters! It was not right! Sam felt FURIOUS. His letters, his dreams, his world was being invaded. He didn't really mind Spitfire being there with him, but not Toughie Wilson!

"So," declared Spitfire firmly, "we need to find out what's going on."

"What do you mean?"

"We'll go up there tonight," she announced, "and find out."

Chapter 8

Cat Burglars

They had taken the dogs back to the Colonel's and he insisted they stop for tea and cakes.

"Perhaps Toughie's got a telescope," whispered Spitfire while the Colonel was piling up plates of food, "or a phone tap… or he's bugging our computers." Her mouth was pulled in small and tight and her eyes flashed, "Oh…I don't know what, but he's spying on us, isn't he? And I don't like spies. I'm not sharing my dreams with *him*."

"Yes…but…?" Sam faltered.

"So, tonight it won't take us long to get there if we use that path over the field in front of the canal pub. Make sure you have your camera inside your jacket. We'll pretend we are going to karate and then…" she broke off as the Colonel turned back towards them. Sam said nothing; he was going to have to go along with this totally mad, bad, plan or make feeble excuses as to why he did not want to venture out in the dark to –well, to do what? What did she think they could achieve?

"Oh, those look fab. Come on Sam, we'll need lots of energy for tonight – for karate –I mean."

Sam stared at the amazingly beautiful cakes and seriously wondered if adventures were a good idea. Only a couple of months ago, his gran's rabbit-warren flat, his dad's pale cream duplex, and the Colonel's safe secure rocket had been his world. Now he was surrounded by dogs, canals, karate, motorbikes, secret cameras, weird messages on glittering paper, fantastic dreams and this mad curly-haired idiot expecting him to go up to Toughie Wilson's house in the dead of night.

But at seven that evening he was there, shivering with fear, outside the hall, as Spitfire ran down the road. She was late. She was always late and oh, what a relief, she had Custard with her!

"Look, I don't know what you've got in mind, but are you really sure this is a good idea?" he muttered, Spitfire didn't even notice.

"We've got an hour and a half. It will take us twenty minutes to get there, twenty minutes to get back here. That will give us a whopping forty minutes to case the joint. Toughie's dad always goes to the pub after he has dropped Toughie off here and his mum goes to Bingo, so the place will be empty."

"What if we get caught?"

"Clever, careful, crafty people don't get caught," she replied firmly. "Come on Sam, do you want to be dreaming the same dreams as Toughie Wilson?" That clinched it. They were his dreams, his letters; he was not sharing them with Toughie Wilson.

It actually took them twenty-five minutes to get there. Ten of those minutes were through the wood. After perhaps twenty steps into the trees, all the light from the street lamps seemed to have been doused by the tangled branches overhead and big gnarled roots lay across the path, which they couldn't see anyhow. Sam had a nasty suspicion that they were actually walking round in circles when, suddenly, there they were. They had reached a tall stone wall.

There was one thing Sam had always been able to do really well: he could climb. Toes jammed into the tiny crevices, and fingers reaching out for hand-holds, within seconds he had clambered to the top.

"We'll tie our karate belts together," he said, sitting astride the stone capping, "and then you shove Custard up to me and after that, hang on to your end of the belt while I pull you up. OK?"

Once on the other side, Spitfire whispered, "We'll take Custard round the outside of the house, just outside the security light zone so there is a strange dog smell everywhere. Then we'll shove her back over the wall, come back and throw a couple of rocks as far as we can across the lawn. That should trigger the lights. The dogs will dash out and they'll pick up Custard's smell and go careering around barking like mad, setting off all the alarms and in all that confusion, we might see a way into the house."

"What if we don't?" he asked doubtfully.

"We'll think of something else," Spitfire declared. They cautiously crept down towards the lawn, through the circle of shrubs.

Sam was not convinced; he was not at all convinced, but he couldn't think of anything, let alone a better idea.

But it worked; seconds after they had lobbed a couple of rocks onto the lawn, the lights sprung on, and three Rottweilers exploded from the front door. Suddenly the grounds around the house were bathed in bright white light, as the dogs dashed straight towards where they were hiding. Like a punch in the stomach, Sam felt the panic hit him. Spitfire bent down, grabbed another stone, and flung it as hard as she could towards the bushes on the opposite side of the lawn.

"Get 'em boys! Go on! Bite their bums!" shouted a big, stocky man dressed in a vest and overalls.

"Oh Glory Hallelujah! I'd forgotten about the handyman." breathed Spitfire. The man strolled out onto the lawn. "There, Rudolf, over there!" yelled the man, running towards the bushes at the other side of the lawn, leaving the door behind him wide open.

"Run Sam!" ordered Spitfire, shoving him forward into the glare of the spotlights. What else could he do but run, his legs wobbling with terror? Seconds later he had reached the door, was inside and there was Spitfire behind him. She turned and, with one swift movement, dragged the door shut. They heard the click of the lock fall into place.

They were locked in - the guard was locked out.

"Quick," Spitfire whispered. "There are two of them I think – he has a wife, but it will take them a bit of time to work out what has happened. We'd better get lost before anyone else comes this way."

Two of them! She had not mentioned three dogs and now there were two grown-ups as well. Sam fumbled in his pocket for the switch of the camera, his hands trembling. Good, it was on.

He was surprised how nice it was inside. It all looked just like any ordinary, if very large and very wealthy house: hall, dining room, lounge, TV room, games room, cloakroom, office.

"What are we actually looking for?" Sam whispered. They had been tiptoeing from room to room, silently, always waiting for the commotion to start when the man outside discovered that he was locked out, always ready to dart behind the long floor-length curtains.

"Clues, of course!" Spitfire hissed back at him. He had just opened a door at the end of the corridor, when what they had been dreading occurred. There was a horrendous banging.

"Oi, Rosa, Rosa? Where are you? Come and open up! The door banged shut behind me. Rosa! Wake up, you great sausage." And behind them they heard a clattering and mumbling; presumably Rosa stumbling along the corridor towards them.

"Quick Spitfire! In here, on the floor, under that table." Sam hissed and seconds later they were both on the floor, almost strangled by wires and plugs, and surrounded by the buzz and hum of computers. Above all that he could hear his own heart thumping and pounding in his chest. The shuffling slippered footsteps were getting closer and closer. She would hear him breathing. He held his breath.

"OK, OK! Coming! Gets himself locked out and then yells at me." The sound of walking stopped. She was outside their door. Spitfire stopped breathing as well. "Oh My Gawd! And look! Now we have the door to the computer room open. Boss will string me up from a tree if he sees that." The children heard the door behind them slam shut. "I'll get this door locked when I've dealt with Good King Wenceslas out there in the cold." And they heard her stump off down the corridor towards the back door.

Locked! They would be locked in.

Spitfire swung her pencil torch in an arc around her head. The room looked as though it was absolutely full of computers – modern technology of the highest degree.

Sam gasped when he saw one screen. It was glowing softly and on it he could see Colonel Quwarndon's web page. He leaned forward and positioned the tiny camera's lens so that it could read the screen. There was a heading '**S I L**' and underneath it the words '**Highest security rating**'. Was this what they were looking for? This must be the clue, this room full of computers; perhaps these computers were connected to the one he had in his bedroom at home; perhaps it was connected to Spitfire's computer. Could a computer make them all dream the same dream? Was that possible?

He felt a tiny spark of pleasure. This was the clue. But now they had discovered it, they didn't have even a minute in which to investigate further. They had to get out of that room before they were locked in.

Chapter 9

Karate King

The moment the corridor outside the room was quiet, they swung open the door, listened, and then, swift as squirrels, quiet as moths, they flew down the corridor.

"There'll be a back door; she's gone to the front door, we will be able to…" started Spitfire. The door at the end of the corridor was open, it lead into a huge kitchen full of big heavy, old-fashioned appliances, making the whole place look almost like a school kitchen. "Look, that must be the back door." The keys were in the lock.

Seconds later they were outside, across a concreted yard, behind a parked Volvo, over a small wall, and into the pool of darkness. Oh, wonderful deep darkness! Not so long before, Sam had hated being outside in the dark at night, but now the dark made him invisible; dark was safe.

It took them five minutes to reach the perimeter

wall and this time even Spitfire climbed it. And then they ran non-stop, with gasping breath and wobbling legs, Custard lolloping along beside them. Not a word was spoken until they reached the dark comforting safety of the karate hall, and slid down in the corridor, their backs against the wall, legs out-stretched across the floor.

"That was great." declared Spitfire and then started to giggle, relieved exhausted giggles. "Just look at your lovely white karate gear. You're filthy, your gran will..." but she got no further, for the door behind them had swung open and Mr. Wilson, just a little shaky on his feet was staggering towards them.

"Kids everywhere! Under your feet, in your hair, under your beds next, I suppose. Out of the way, brats!" he growled as he blundered past.

Out of school the next day, the sun shone and the gentle wind whipped his red hair up into a crest. Sam was pleased with himself. He was an accomplished cat burglar who could scale high walls, confuse dangerous guard dogs, hide from resident caretakers, discover hidden secrets and escape undetected. He danced off down the street, leaping over obstacles, swinging his school bag with reckless abandon. He had completely forgotten about the crumpled scrap of paper with its half-understood message about the red shrimp. Anyhow, he was ready for anything and anybody.

He had just got to the dull bit of the walk home. It was a short plain street of terraced houses where there never seemed to be anyone around. Sleeping houses closed in on themselves, their windows tight-shut like blind eyes. He was so full of himself that he had not noticed two older boys lurking at the end of the road, and he was blissfully unaware of the third, slowly creeping up towards him from behind, until it was almost too late. Suddenly he sensed something strange in the two lads slowly advancing towards him, heads down, arms by their sides, hoods pulled over their faces. Sam stopped, quickly glanced over his shoulder and caught sight of the third figure. Just one glance was enough to tell him; it was Toughie himself.

Sam felt every ounce of confidence drain from him. Now limp with fear, he grasped the one tool left to him; the plan he had worked out a few days earlier. Hi Lo had told him exactly what to do. Hi Lo and his grandmother, the two of them, together leaning up against the peeling gym wall, one evening after karate.

"Surprise, Sam, surprise! That is the key to success. Don't stop to think whether this will work; just do it."

"Just do it, Sam." His grandmother had repeated.

OK he would just do it. One quick breath, then first the run straight towards the two older boys in front of him, until he was practically within arm's reach. Then the almighty leap to one side, so that he was just to the right of them. Next, three steps forward again. Now he was behind them and ready to swivel round and dive down as hard and fast as he could, straight into the back of the knees of the nearest boy.

A blur of arms and legs. He had done exactly

what he had been told to do, landing like a slab of concrete against the back of Spike's knees.

"Guu...ur...ur," Spike gasped as he toppled forwards and sideways, knocking hard into Jaz as he tumbled down. There they were, the two of them on the ground, an untidy pile of heads and feet and shoulders and elbows.

"Keep your arms up, bounce back on to your feet, turn and face the next one," he could hear Hi Lindly's voice in his head.

"Turn and face the next one," intoned his gran.

"Don't pull the pin out of that safety alarm we gave you Sam, until you have it pressed against his head, just above the ear."

"Above the ear, Sam," Gran repeated earnestly.

Sam spun round; Toughie was almost upon him, so he sprang forward, straight into Toughie's amazed face, dragged his alarm from his pocket, and clamped it against Toughie's cheekbone. He pulled out the pin. The horrendous wail echoed down the street.

"Owww...Owww..." yelled Toughie, bent double as the hideous row hammered into his brain.

"Don't let go Sam, no matter what they do to you,

slide the alarm round until you can push it down the back of the neck under their shirt, and then just drop it and run."

"Back of the neck, Sam!" echoed his gran firmly.

Sam did exactly what they had told him to do, pushing the alarm in, so that it was screaming and wailing right next to Toughie's spine. He stood back; Toughie had collapsed on top of the other two and was desperately scrabbling at his sweatshirt. Breathing hard, Sam added his own touch to the plan: three sharp kicks directed at the boys' legs before he turned and ran helter-skelter down the road. Fear, excitement and pride giving wings to his feet.

He had beaten three boys at one go. Three boys, older and stronger than he was. Perhaps they would try again but he had escaped unharmed. He wasn't lying curled up on the road, being kicked, begging for mercy. He felt OK. He felt great.

Ten minutes later, Colonel Quwarndon was silently studying the footage he had taken of the assault with his secret camera. "I think we need some assistance with all this, we need some more troops to tackle this problem. Let me just get a copy of this episode, so we can show it to the police."

Sam passed the camera over. He was very tired and a bit scared. Maybe the grown-ups would make it all too difficult. He leant back and closed his eyes. Now that it was all over he felt weak.

"Sam?" Colonel Quwarndon was standing next to one of the computer screens, and Sam realised with a shock that showing on the screen, was the view of the inside of the house that he and Spitfire had burgled the night before. Of course, he had forgotten: the footage of everything that he and Spitfire had done on the previous night, was still on the camera.

Chapter 10

The Gathering of the Clan

The Colonel watched the film in silence, from the start where they had climbed over the wall right through to when they got back to the gym hall, followed by the incident with Toughie, Spike and Jaz, and then he rewound the film and watched it all from the very beginning all over again. Finally he turned to look at Sam.

"Well?" he asked very, very quietly.

Sam rubbed his knees, chewed the inside of his lips and felt himself shrink to the size of a walnut. "It all started with the dream, when we realized that all three of us had had the same dream, " he muttered.

"Dream?" queried the Colonel, his forehead wrinkled like a rhino skin.

"Spitfire and me, we had identical dreams, and Toughie Wilson. All of us had the same dream. It was so odd; we had different dreams but there were identical words in them. Words about the back of the canal next to an open field."

Colonel Quwarndon's face had turned in a few seconds from being very slightly angry, to that of extreme anxiousness. He sat down abruptly.

"Say that again, slowly. Explain exactly what you mean." So Sam told him about his own dream, how he had discovered that Spitfire was dreaming the same words and how she had found out that Toughie Wilson had dreamt the same thing.

The Colonel, looking very, very serious, leant forward. "Don't tell this story to anyone, anyone at all; not even your grandmother. Tell her about Toughie Wilson and his bullyboys trying to beat you up, tell her how the advice that she and Hi Lo gave you worked like a charm, but nothing else. Tell her not to go to the police – not yet. I have some very serious work to do on my computer. But come straight here from school tomorrow and bring Spitfire with you. Right?"

Sam nodded; he had never seen the Colonel quite so serious before.

All that evening Sam worried.

The Colonel had discovered that he had broken

into someone's house. He and Spitfire were guilty of breaking and entering – the Colonel would tell his father and his father would tell the police. What would they do? It was impossible to even imagine what would happen after that. Perhaps they'd all have to go and see the Wilsons. Perhaps the Wilsons would charge them with trespassing, or breaking and entering. Not that they had actually broken anything. Nobody would even notice the fight. That was just kids quarrelling, wasn't it? And he was the one who had inflicted the most injury. He'd get told off for that.

Before he fell asleep, he pulled the treasure box out from under the bed, and took out the folded papers, all three of them, shimmering, glorious papers with mysterious magical letters. But he put those unopened on the duvet and carefully lifted the cards – the cards that appeared each year beside his plate on his birthday. Quite ordinary cards, except that inside there would be a short rhyme. Last year's was 'Eight! Not too early, not too late, you ride as high as a King in state.'

"What does 'in state' mean, Dad? " he had asked.

"You know, it means grand, like a king." Sam

had been very impressed. But it was the last word on the card, which was the most important bit.

Mum.

Written, big and bold, with a long dash underneath the letters. Sam looked at the card for a long time before wrapping it back in the little bit of tissue paper, as he always did.

It was two very quiet children who walked slowly home from school the next afternoon. They opened the door, and climbed the rope ladder. There were no welcoming smells of recently baked cakes as there usually was. The computer space was littered all over with half-filled coffee cups and, as they entered, the Colonel and his dad were both there, each huddled over a keyboard clicking away like mad.

His dad glanced over one shoulder. "Just sit down for a minute you two," he said and Sam's heart, already rock bottom, fell even lower, and then turning to the Colonel, he continued:

"Yes, I think you are right, Colonel. This man has no obvious means of making money but is extraordinarily rich, so the cash has to come from somewhere;

but from where and how, that is the question."

"Exactly! Right, you two." Both men swivelled their chairs round to face the two children. Sam felt his heart freeze. Now for the big telling-off. No more karate. Jelly, back to the Dogs' Home. Grounded for a month. He waited for it all to explode around him.

"It seems, almost by chance," the Colonel started," that you two have stumbled on a very serious criminal. Fairly recently, somebody has been hacking into my computer and has managed to copy all the details of an amazingly powerful technique that I discovered when I was as army scientist. It's called '**SIL**' which has top security rating. I had a suspicion a few days ago that one of my programs had been tampered with, but I was not absolutely sure."

He paused for a moment and then continued, "Your father and I, we believe that we have tracked him down and it seems he is very wealthy, has a company in his name, but makes nothing, does nothing, buys and sells nothing."

His dad took up the story, "But he seems to be using his computers all the time, and he seems to be making money – lots of money. And he has the ability to hack into any computer, anywhere. And now he has discovered how to secretly put powerful suggestions into peoples' minds."

Sam was not entirely sure if he understood what they were telling him, but Spitfire, as quick as lightning, had seen what it was all leading up to.

"Ah! Oh! So if he put a suggestion into the mind of a bank manager, something like: the bank manager was to take two million pounds out of the bank and put that money into this man's own bank account and then put the suggestion in the bank manager's mind to run away, or something like that, then it would look like..." she trailed off.

"It would look like the bank manager had stolen the money and had run away with it. Yes, exactly." Sam's father completed the sentence.

"And he can do all that just from sitting at home in front of his computer, so no one would even know he had been in contact with the bank manager at all. In fact he could just tell the police he had been at home, feeding the goldfish all the time this was going on," continued the Colonel.

"Wow! " said Sam. "Can you find out who this

man is?"

"That's what we two have been doing all day and we think we have tracked him down to this house." The Colonel clicked the mouse arrow on Google Earth. The computer screen swung into focus, slowly coming to rest over a large house, surrounded by a wall, a wood, and below it a field, a road and a canal. Sam and Spitfire stared at the screen; they could even see the path across the field up through the wood, to the place where they had climbed over the wall the previous night.

"Toughie Wilson's house?" breathed Spitfire.

"All those computers we saw, the one showing your web page, Colonel, was it from there that he does all those clever things?" The two men nodded; both looked extremely serious.

Sam began to think that they were not going to get the blasting he had feared. Perhaps by chance, as the Colonel had said, they had actually stumbled on a master criminal after all.

"So, on the strength of what you two discovered the night before last, we are thinking that we might be able to stop Mr. Wilson's little game before it gets out of hand. Your video showed us the layout of the garden, the plan of the house, and the computer system." He stopped, got up and strode to the fridge, took out a large slice of cheese, grabbed a bite and shoved it back into the fridge.

"Action! Action! We have got to move fast; very fast. This man is clever, so he will use what he got from me straight away." The Colonel seemed unsure as to whether to open the fridge door again or not. "Tonight, yes, tonight, we will have to strike," he declared in a military voice which clashed a bit with his faded pale blue shorts, sandalled feet and purple striped rugby shirt – and the crumbs of cheese on his chin.

"And so, " said Sam's dad," you two will have to do your bit. We have already called in all the troops...Good! That sounds like them. Let them in Sam."

Sam blinked – troops? Strike? Tonight? Bemused, he slid down the escape pole leading to the front door. Opening it, he saw firstly Beryl the Magnificent holding the leads of both Jelly and Custard; behind her stood Aunt Lucy, wearing dirty green overalls with 'Bob's best Potatoes' embroidered on the front and back, and finally, his grandmother in what looked like gypsy fancy dress costume. She had huge gold earrings, a black wig and a flounced red skirt.

"Right," boomed Beryl, sweeping past him. "When do we start?"

Chapter 11

Helicopters, Tennis Balls and Gypsies

With military thoroughness, the Colonel had planned everything.

Beryl and Spitfire were to control the guard dogs. "Letitia, I want you to put your fortune-telling skills into practice and keep Rosa and perhaps Marko absorbed. Lucy, what have you got as transport for us?"

"I've borrowed the potato delivery van from the chap next door. You will all have to bring a cushion because the metal floor is a bit hard and very dirty," she replied.

"You'll be the nerve centre of the whole operation and I want you parked up in a lay-by some distance from the house itself," the Colonel continued before turning to Sam:

"And Sam, you and me, we are going to have to get into the house and disable the computers." Sam hardly dared to breathe; back into the house a second time; his heart was already thumping inside his chest.

"And, Jeffery," the Colonel turned to Sam's dad. "You have the trickiest job of all. Distraction!"

"Distraction?" asked Sam.

"He must confuse the Wilson family," suggested Lucy.

"How? " asked Sam.

The Colonel and his father both smiled, self-satisfied, small, happy little grins.

"Helicopter landing," said his father quietly.

Beryl whistled, Lucy laughed and Sam felt his jaw drop open. Spitfire's eyes were the size of golf balls.

"And listen folks, we'll have to wait until it's dark, so we need a good hearty meal. No drinks, all right?" declared the Colonel.

"No drinks?" roared Beryl.

"Can't have my troops desperate for the loo halfway through an exercise!" barked the Colonel. The following hour was almost a party. Gran had brought with her a huge saucepan of vegetable soup, which they ate while discussing enthusiastically what they were about to do.

"Here Spitfire, put these tennis balls in your pocket," whispered Beryl. She and Spitfire were crouched down behind a bush at the back of the property, just outside the security light zone.

"Tennis balls?" Spitfire had wondered if she had heard properly.

"We want the dogs to play, don't we? Guard dogs get so little chance to chase balls. They just love it if you throw balls for them. But you must not run after any ball they miss. Just lob another one."

"OK" Spitfire had replied, not entirely sure about the idea. "But we have got to keep them quiet for forty minutes! Will they play ball for that long?"

"Of course not, we just keep going until they are really relaxed and friendly, then I will hypnotise them."

"Hypno..." she never managed to finish the sentence as the lights all around the house blazed into action, and she saw the bent figure of an old woman, stumbling down the drive towards the house. It was Sam's grandmother (over-acting as usual); Spitfire could even hear that she was singing to herself in a wavering voice.

Further round, towards the back of the house Sam crouched down and watched as his gran approached the side door. She pounded on the door with her stick. Seconds later it was open and the dogs streaked out, barking loudly as they careered out across the lawn.

Beryl rolled a ball across the grass and said, firmly but quietly, "Fetch boy, fetch." The dog stopped, turned, saw the ball and scurried off after it. Spitfire forgot her doubts and rolled out her ball, "Fetch boy, fetch!" It worked. Both dogs grabbed their balls and trotted quietly up to them, ready for the next throw. Deep in the shrubbery, Sam and the Colonel waited, they could just about hear the conversation going on at the side of the house:

"Well?" barked Marko, glaring at the crumpled-looking gypsy in front of him.

"Oh, you must come from Transgovia," that was his gran's wavery voice. "Perhaps even from Eskevey. The way you say 'well'. The way your eyes flash. The way you stand. Even the way you hold your hands. The men from that part of the world always hold their hands like that." Gran imitated a big, strong man's fist

(The Colonel had done a lot of research on the Internet; he knew exactly where both Marko and his wife Rosa, had come from).

Marko stepped back, "Well?" he said again, but his tone was very different this time.

"I am Madame Petrolinnia. I read the cards; I look into the future." She paused, and dropped her voice to a breathy whisper, "I read palms and tea leaves, and I carry messages from… from…from your loved ones on the other side. Perhaps your wife would let me tell her fortune."

Marko stood silent, unsure, but Rosa was already at his side; she had heard everything.

"And me, where do I come from? If you're so clever?" she demanded.

Gran peered up at the woman, silently. She leaned forward a little, and then rocked back on her heels. "Well, I think, yes, I think you must be from…Rochdale... No… no… a village outside Rochdale … But I'm not sure which." Rosa let out a great burst of laughter.

"Come on in, let's see what you can do. Better than watching the telly." The side door slammed shut, leaving the guard dogs outside, everyone else inside.

"Lucy?" the Colonel whispered into his mobile, "So far so good. The dogs are quiet – Letitia's in the house – Rosa seems keen."

"Fine," crackled Lucy's voice over the phone, "I'll check and see how Beryl's getting on with the dogs."

Spitfire had watched in amazement as, while she continued to play a quiet ball-rolling game with the big brown dog, Beryl had already got the second dog's face held between her rough hands while she gazed deep into its eyes murmuring, "Sleepy, sleepy. Sleepy time, lie down, tummy tickles, tummy tickle," as the big animal, giving a deep sigh, sagged forward.

Sam heard the phone click and Lucy's whispered words:

"OK Colonel, Let phase two commence." It seemed to Sam that only minutes later, they heard what they all had been waiting for: first it was a low grumble, followed by an ever-increasing roar as the helicopter drew ever closer. Finally, there was a deafening racket as it slowly circled the house.

Once round the chimneys, twice, three times – by the third time, all the outside lights had flashed back on and the three Wilsons, father, mother and son, as well as Marko had erupted out of the front door and were gazing in amazed fascination up at the sky.

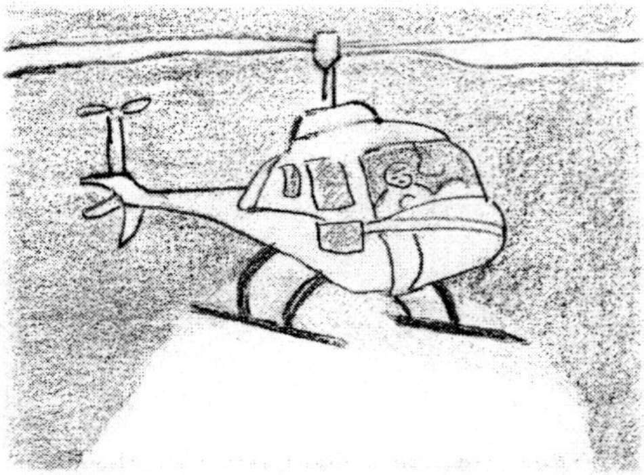

At that point his dad had flicked a couple of switches, the helicopter coughed and the engine stopped dead. For a few heart-stopping seconds it seemed to be hanging silently in mid-air, ready to drop like a stone. But just moments later, the engines re-started, the helicopter hovered over the front lawn and then slowly, slowly, the blades flashing round in a spinning circle above, it descended until it finally came to rest in front of the house.

"Now," whispered the Colonel and he and Sam ran like greyhounds towards the back door. Even as the Colonel was fiddling with his special key, (a skeleton key which can open any door), Sam's dad was struggling out of the helicopter.

"Sorry, so sorry… Taking this old bucket of rust up to Scotland for a mate. He said I might have to ditch once or twice. Just have to reset the squander tappets, if they get too hot. Sorry about your lawn. Rest assured, we will reimburse you for any damage to this lovely turf." He stood smiling a slow, gentle, slightly quizzical smile.

"Name's Burton, madam. Avery Burton," he added, extending his hand towards Mrs. Wilson. "Will you lend me your handsome husband and fine lad here for a few minutes? If I have someone to help, the whole job should only take a tick." The Wilsons, en masse, were won over and it was obvious that Marko was not going to be left out, either.

"Just need someone to hold tight on to the fuel pipe, while we straighten out…" And within minutes everyone was clutching onto wires, pipes, or tools, while Sam's dad, dashed to each in turn, screwing, twisting, or bending, murmuring encouragement to each one in turn.

Inside the house all the lights were on, the sound of a telly boomed out from one of the rooms and a strong smell of fish and chips seemed to hang in the air. Sam was even more scared than he had been the first time they had been in the house. He felt sure that someone, anyone, was going to stroll out of one of the rooms and demand an explanation as to why they were there. None of this seemed to worry the Colonel.

"Down this corridor, I think," he murmured, "turn to the left and take the third door down. Aha! Here we are." They had reached the computer room.

"Oh, dear me," whispered the Colonel, "I thought there were only six computers, there are eight here and I have to check each one. Forty minutes if I give each five minutes. We said we'd be out in thirty-five minutes. Let's get to work."

Sam started up each computer; the Colonel followed behind him, clicking like mad, while Sam hovered behind, closing down each in turn. It took them twenty-four desperate minutes.

"Last job, Sam; how much longer have we got?"

"Eleven minutes Colonel."

"Alright Sam – every single plug has got to be taken out and this little black disc has to be clicked into the socket and the plugs put back. Get to work."

The room was full of plugs. Sam's fingers flew.

Pull out the plugs, shove in the disc, plug back. Pull out, shove in, plug back, over and over again. It was all going to plan.

The Colonel's mobile phone buzzed, "Colonel, you have one minute; *one minute only*. Get out of there!"

Outside they could hear the helicopter roar into life, at the same time there was a frantic yapping from the dogs, and in amongst the entire row they heard Sam's grandmother say in an unnaturally loud voice, " And, my dear, here are just a few of my cards; ask your friends if they would like a visit from Madame Petrolinnia."

At the back door, the dogs were scrabbling noisily. At the side door Rosa was saying a grateful goodbye to Grandmother. Swarming around the front door, the Wilson clan, plus Marko, were waving frantically towards the receding helicopter.

No way out through the front door!

Rosa was at the side door! No way out there!

No way out by the back door where the dogs were yelping. Never before had Sam realized that panic created real pain in your body. It flowed like a sharp wire down his arms and legs. They were trapped.

There was no way of escape.

They had left it too late!

Chapter 12

Nursery Rhymes

Fear hurts. Sam's heart thumped so hard, it bruised his ribs and shook up his stomach, it stopped his breath and it paralysed his brain. He could not think. He could not move, but at the same time he was trembling so badly it was hard to stand up. They were trapped halfway down the corridor, which led from the kitchen on to the side door and finally to the front door.

Sam couldn't even turn his head to see if anyone was entering the corridor. He could not move his head, or his eyes, or feet. And then:

"Excuse me, ma'am, I'll just pop back out the front door and call up those dogs – maybe the helicopter spooked them." Marko's voice boomed out loud and clear.

It was obvious. He was going to go back out of the front door to bellow for the dogs, which meant they would scamper away from the back door, leaving it free.

And Sam discovered that indeed he could not only move, he could almost fly. Down into the kitchen they clattered, over to the back door, still unlocked, across the brilliant, white sheet of lawn, crashing into the jumbled bushes beyond, over the wall, stumbling and tripping over the brambles and undergrowth of the coal-black wood and finally to the van.

"Drive!" yelled the Colonel when he saw that Grandmother, Spitfire and Beryl were already there, scrunched up on the dirty, earthy floor of the van. Sam collapsed in amongst them. He was shivering violently. With cold? With fear? With relief? He did not know which, just that his whole body was out of his control.

Back at last, at the Colonel's, his father was already calmly waiting for them all. There were mugs of coffee and hot chocolate ready for everyone. The white, gently buzzing interior of the Colonel's rocket base seemed the safest place in the whole world. Behind the ordinary plain front door, up the rope ladder and into the shiny computer space, he was safe at last. His heart slowed down. He could breathe; how long had he been holding his breath?

Then everyone had a chance to tell their tale - what had happened – how they had done what they had to do.

"I told Rosa she would win the lottery. She believed me!" chuckled Gran.

"I told the dogs they were really, really sleepy. They believed me!" crowed Beryl.

"I told Toughie he should contact me tomorrow for a job as an apprentice engineer." His dad grinned.

"You had a bit of a boring job, Lucy, sitting there in the van all that time," said Gran.

"Oh yes, indeed," replied Lucy, "that was until the police turned up."

There was a sudden hush, as their faces turned to Lucy; "Police?" breathed Spitfire.

"Yes, he drove past once, a few seconds later he cruised past a second time, and on the third attempt, this policeman parked up level with me, poked his head out and says, 'Everything OK, love?' "

"What did you say?" asked Sam.

"Well I wasn't going to tell him that two children, two pensioners, an airline official and a dog handler were trying to break into the local mansion, was I? So I said I needed time to think."

"That satisfied him?" Gran asked in surprise.

"Oh yes, he said, 'Trouble at home, dear? Let me tell you about trouble'. And indeed he did – he was having trouble with his wife, his teenage sons, his mother-in-law, his boss and his dog."

"Poor Man!" interrupted Gran. "I hope you offered some sort of comfort."

"Well, I was going to, when he started on his allotment – it seems there was carrot fly, potato blight and something dreadful attacking the onions. And it was then that I realized I had to give you all the 'FIVE MINUTES TO GET OUT' warning, and he was still sitting there in my passenger seat, eating my toffees." The whole group were gazing at Lucy in amazement.

"So I told him that I had to feed my turkey chicks every four hours and that if I didn't get back home in five minutes, they would all be dead. He leapt out of the van and was gone. That was why I was so late in warning you, Colonel."

"Well, done Lucy," said the Colonel and then with a faint smile he continued, "I checked every computer and every single one was connected up either to a bank or some huge property dealer, or a mobile phone company, or something like that. He was meddling in business deals across the world and just sucking up money wherever or whenever he wanted to."

"And did you wipe all his computers clean, so that he can't steal any more information or money?" asked Spitfire.

"No, I left each computer just as he had set them up." He paused.

"What?" yelled Beryl, "I spent forty minutes lying on wet grass gazing into the eyes of the smelliest dog I have ever met for nothing!"

The Colonel grinned a truly wicked grin. "But the moment he switches on anything at all in that room, it will activate a little device I slipped into the plugs. The computers will start up all right and then they will begin playing nursery rhymes – fifty nursery rhymes, sung by a lady with a high watery voice, one after the other. And when they have finished, they'll start all over again. Even if he finally tracks down the device hidden in the plugs and removes it, all eight computers will have been reprogrammed to do nothing but play nursery rhymes.

Beryl was the first to laugh. "Sung by a lady with a high watery voice!"

Sam was, by then, laughing so hard that his head began to throb. "And his printers? What about those?" asked Grandmother, wiping the tears of laughter from her cheeks.

"Yes, they will print nursery rhymes, and his fax machine and his telephones, they will play nursery rhymes. And I got back all the **SIL** data he had stolen from my computer, so my secret technique is safe." murmured the Colonel. "Congratulations team! We have averted a major criminal attack on any one of the world's banks. You did a really good job tonight. And Jeffrey, you'd better take that borrowed helicopter back to its rightful owner."

Grandmother glanced across at Sam, still shivering, his fingers wrapped tightly around his cup of hot chocolate.

"Sam? You look terrible!" She crossed the room, her hand already stretched towards his forehead. "Good heavens! You have a temperature – we'd better get you into bed."

Chapter 13

Flu is Horrible

Sam didn't know flu could be so horrible.

All he wanted to do was to be left to lie there, and not move any part of him at all. Indeed, not moving was all he did for the next week. He just lay there, coughing, sneezing, first too hot and then too cold and feeling as weak as a caterpillar. Too tired to read, too tired to talk, too tired to turn over.

Beryl volunteered to walk Jelly. And his dad fussed and flapped and worried in a way Sam had never noticed before, although now that he thought about it, he remembered how dad had always panicked when he was ill. Meanwhile, Spitfire came every other day to update him with news from school.

"Toughie Wilson has been off school for the last four days."

"Mmm," Sam managed to murmur.

"And everybody says that the Wilsons have sold all their cars; all three of them."

"Really," Sam whispered.

"And they say the caretaker and cook have been sacked; that must be Marko and Maria. And when are you getting better? I'm bored with walking Custard by myself."

But it took Sam much longer to get better than he had expected; as the first week of sickness ran into a second, he was still too weak to get up.

At last he began to regain his strength. First he went back to school and restarted karate, but what he really wanted, was to get back to the wood and to search for more letters, more scraps of shiny paper, more weird messages.

It was not to be. While the brown crunchy leaves that had carpeted the floor had now been blown away and fresh green shoots started to appear, still he found nothing. Perhaps it was desperation that drove him to carry on searching. He peered into hollow tree stumps, behind mossy rocks, under the green tent of holly twigs, but after a bit he stopped looking. After all the excitement life, had become dull.

It was half term; Spitfire had gone away to stay

with some distant cousin in the country. The Colonel was visiting a nephew. Lucy could not take him climbing or kayaking because she had had to go and report on a race in Italy; Dad was on a three week stint of flying in India and his grandmother had decided the light of her life, at that very moment, was to make marmalade, so now she had no time or energy left for anything else. Beryl, however, had been made temporary manager of the Dogs' Home, and she suggested Sam could go there and help a bit.

At first, all he did was washing out the food bowls. Then he was allowed to walk batches of the smaller dogs, to comb the hair of the longer-haired cats, and to see that the lizards had warm water.

They both discovered that if Jelly was kept in the small animal zone, she was perfectly happy to trail around on her own. She would gently push her nose against the wire of the hutch containing hamsters or gerbils, and as she had never been a cat chaser, she even seemed to make friends with the cats. She still found the howling and barking of the large dogs in the compound upsetting, but in with the smaller animals she was completely at ease and was allowed to wander wherever she wanted to.

Beryl treated Sam as a proper assistant. So that afternoon, there he was leaning on a broom, having just swept up most of the sawdust which seemed to cover all the pathways between the cages, when Beryl appeared with a huge mug of hot tea.

"Thought you needed a bit of refreshment, m'lad," she boomed. It was difficult to think of Beryl's speech as anything but booming, it was always so loud and cheerful, except when she was talking to the animals, when she almost sang to them. "Keep up the good work. Every little helps."

Grinning, Sam took the mug of tea and put it down on a bale of straw and started to sweep with renewed energy and pleasure.

He looked back at the clean, swept path behind him and turned the corner into the small animals unit and there was Jelly, big loopy Jelly, trotting up to him with a scrap of black fabric hanging from her mouth.

"Here Jelly, drop girl, drop!"

It turned out to be a small velvet bag, almost a pouch, with a drawstring cord at the top. He fumbled clumsily, trying to see if there was anything inside. His

fingers felt a crumpled scrap of folded paper. It was a slip of sparkling paper; hexagons that seemed to shimmer with every colour of the rainbow as you looked at them; the paper itself flecked with stardust and on the other side, the plain white paper side, there were the letters:

He Ne Ar

And now his delight and pleasure were complete. The letters! His letters had come back. How he had missed them; the tingling thrill of finding them; the way they seemed to create, all on their own, special dreams; how they seemed to explode into his life. Tonight he would dream, he was sure of that – after all it was after he had found: **Be Mg Ca Sr Ba Ra** that he found Jelly. He went to Karate after finding: **H Li Na K** and finally he and Spitfire had found the hidden path up to the Wilson's house after finding: **B C N O F**. So what did these new letters mean?

He Ne Ar

He couldn't ask the Colonel because he was away. Gran was ankle-deep in making marmalade. All the others were away as well. He wasn't sure if he really wanted to tell Beryl; she was, after all, so very sensible and she didn't know about the other letters. He decided that he would go home early and try to work things out by himself. Sam said the letters over and over to himself as he got his jacket and then hurried through to the office.

Beryl was on the phone when he got there and she just nodded and smiled, "Yes, go on Sam, off you go…yes I know, Mr. Johnson…help never arrived …I should never have let him take the …" The rest of the conversation mumbled on.

Help **ne**ver **ar**rived.

He Ne Ar – his letters?

"What did you say?" gasped Sam... "**he**lp **ne**ver

arrived?"

"What?" asked Beryl, already dialling another number. "Yes.... we need sixty tins of..."

He N e A r was it '**H**elp **Ne**ver **Ar**rived' ? No, no those letters could mean anything; they might mean '**He**nry **ne**eds **Ar**madillos'; or '**He**avenly **Ne**w **Ar**ti-chokes' or any number of different meanings. He would have to wait for his dream.

Back in the small animals unit Sam picked up his backpack and started to call, "Jelly! Jelly! JELLY! JELLY?"

She seemed to have disappeared. He called even louder.

He yelled. He searched. No Jelly. He panicked.

Jelly was nowhere to be seen. Frantic with worry, he ran up to one of the other girls helping out. "Have you seen my dog anywhere? You know, the big orange one with floppy hair?"

The girl blew a strand of hair from her face and looked up. "Oh yes, just a moment ago – your friend fetched him for you."

"Fetched him?"

"Yes, he said that because you were staying late,

you wanted him to exercise the dog, so I said OK – go ahead."

"What was he like, this friend of mine?"

"Oh big, with hair stuck up in spikes – look, it was only a moment ago, he's probably still outside…"

Sam knew the description, 'big, with spiky hair!'

Running, dodging, weaving, he dashed to the front entrance. There, screwing up his eyes, he scanned the pavements in both directions.

Yes! There they were. Right down at the end of the road, he could see Jelly quite easily and the big boy, running hard. Even at this distance he could see who it was.

Toughie Wilson had Jelly on a lead and he was running away as fast as he could.

Chapter 14

Kidnapped

Yelling, " Jelly, Jelly!" Sam ran after them. Ran to the end of the road, round the corner and into the thronging mass of cars and people, buses and pushchairs, into the noise and the confusion of an extremely busy road where a boy and a dog can disappear in the shake of a tail. For the next half-hour Sam skidded through the streets, up and down, searching, calling, asking, with an ever-increasing desperation but to no avail.

They had vanished.

Finally, utterly dejected he returned to the Dogs' Home. Beryl's office was empty and the girl he had seen earlier was standing next to the desk. "Beryl's gone out to hunt down some dog food, and I've got to answer the phone and then lock up. Are you going now?"

Sam nodded, too miserable to speak.

Back at his grandmother's flat, the place was

warm bright, quiet and very, very empty. There was an extremely large note stuck on the door of the microwave. His grandmother did this when she was going to be late getting home, and there was a squashy-looking envelope on the floor in the hall. First the note:

FINISHED MAKING THE MARMALADE

SELLING IT AT THE LATE NIGHT

FARMERS MARKET

YOUR TEA IN THE MICROWAVE –

STEAK AND KIDNEY CASSEROLE

Steak and kidney casserole, his favourite, but eating was impossible, sitting down was impossible, and he had to do something.

He picked up the envelope from the hall floor. Inside, was something that made Sam's heart stop beating. It was a sticky mass of fur –Jelly's fur –matted and wet. Wet with something dark reddish-brown.

Blood.

And there was a note.

Had to snip of a bit of its er to get this. Lot of blod in dogs ers. Yu do wat I tel yu, if yu dnt I'l tak of it's paws, I by I til its warking on stumps.

Sam sat on the floor of the hall clutching the little bit of ear to his chest and sobbed, big, dry, hard, painful sobs. Jelly, his darling, lovely, soft, kindly, brave Jelly, and then he re-read the note translating it as he went: 'Had to snip off her ear to get this. Lot of blood in dogs' ears. You do what I tell you, if you don't I'll take off its paws, one by one, till it's walking on stumps.'

At last he stood up, slowly, as if he was no longer a boy; he felt old and cold and afraid. There was nobody, absolutely nobody around to help him. He was going to have to rescue Jelly on his own. He suddenly remembered the letters, **He Ne Ar**, and then the words he had heard Beryl say, '**He**lp **Ne**ver **Ar**rived'. They must have been a message to him in this very situation. Help was not going to arrive; there was only one person who could save Jelly.

In a sort of numb daze, he got ready: leave a note for Gran (she mustn't be worried about him), get a torch, his camera, what else? He couldn't think.

Outside, it was extremely dark with a drizzle of cold rain spitting down. He ran down the road to the canal path, and then skidding and sliding along by the side of the greasy black water in the canal, as far as the pub and across the field to the base of the wood and then stopped.

The streetlights had faded into a smudged, wet blur behind him and the wood was as dark as the tongue in a black cat's mouth; it would swallow him up alive. After two steps under the trees, he stopped. He could feel the twigs grasping, slapping, snatching at his hair; the roots were snagging his feet, the cold shoved wet fingers under his jacket. He just could not go through the wood; not alone; not at night; his torch made no difference. If he could not even get as far as the wall around the house, how was he to rescue Jelly?

"Sam Roberts this is only a wood – it is not alive – this is the same wood you ran through with Spitfire only a few weeks ago." He actually said the words aloud to himself. "It will take you no longer than five minutes to get up to the wall."

He would do just ten steps and see how it was, and then another ten. One…two…three...four…five, six, seven, eight, nine, ten. He had done ten steps, and suddenly realised he had done those ten steps with his eyes closed. He flicked his eyes open.

The dark was not quite as black; more a sort of purple, a menacing, and leering creeping mauve. He snapped his eyes shut and feeling his way forward with hands outstretched he started on the next ten, and then the next. Very quietly he started to sing:

"Ten green bottles hanging on the wall… Ten green bottles hanging on the wall and if one green bottle should accidentally fall, there'll be..." his voice wavering and weak, he stumbled forwards. He had got as far as two green bottles, when suddenly he realised he could see the outline of the wall ahead of him, and the paler slice of sky beyond the wood.

He'd made it. He gave a great sob of relief, and stopped biting his lips quite so tightly.

It took Sam no time at all to scramble over the wall, after which he slowly skirted the whole compound, peering down through the encircling shrubs across the lawn to the house itself. It looked dark and deserted. He had crept nearly round the entire house, when he suddenly heard it. A long mournful howl. The baleful howl of a desperately unhappy dog.

Jelly had to be in one of the double garages at the back of the house; a big solid concrete garage.

The security lights, which guarded the entire house, only shone onto the front doors of the garage; the back was unprotected, unlit. Seconds later, Sam had scampered across the bit of grass at the back and had pressed himself tight into the shadows.

The garage was as secure as a castle: concrete walls, locked metal, up-and-over doors. There was no way in. In utter defeat, Sam sank into a huddled crouch behind it. What could he do? Head shrunk down between his shoulders, he tried to work out a plan. Jelly's long, slow, crying howls sobbed out through the walls into his very bones.

Right, he would go up to the back door, he would knock on the door, Toughie would come and then he would say 'Give me my dog now!' And then he would fight him. Yes, he would. He didn't care if Toughie was taller, stronger, and heavier. He didn't care if he was going to get hurt.

"Shh, shhh … shhhh" Then again. "Shh, shh … shhh."

The sound came from the bushes behind him. He peered up at them. He could see a shopping bag.

A shopping bag!

A foot?

Seconds later the shopping bag, rucksack and his grandmother were there with him, huddled against the shadowed back wall. "How did you know…?" he stuttered. She looked very grim.

"You left the envelope and that note with Jelly's hair, on the floor in the hall. And I put two and two together," she whispered and slightly noisily, started to unpack the shopping bag. "Wire cutters, mallet, sticky-backed plastic, towel, leather gloves; we should manage alright with that lot."

"Sticky-backed plastic?" Sam didn't know

whether to laugh or cry, how does one break into Fort Knox with sticky-backed plastic?

"I'll lean my back against the wall and cup my hands. You stand on my hands, stick the plastic all over the glass in that little window up there, get the mallet out of your pocket, crack the glass in the window, put the gloves on, pull away as much of the glass as you can from the sides, put the towel over the sharp bottom bits and wriggle through.

"Gran, were you a burglar in your previous life?"

Sam managed to follow every one of the instructions, but now Jelly was howling and barking and whining altogether. Surely they could hear it in the house! "Gran I'm going in. I've got to shut Jelly up or we'll be discovered."

He spread the towel over the needle-sharp points of smashed glass still poking up from the putty around the edges. It looked dangerous; it felt murderous; but with his hands over the edge he levered himself up, tipped his shoulders down, and fell head-first into the black open hole and landed on top of a squealing, licking, yelping Jelly.

His grandmother had told him exactly what to

do next. He was supposed to switch on the lights and then photograph Jelly against every wall of the garage, as quickly as possible. As soon as he had done that, he was to find something to stand on and then shove Jelly, as best as he could, through the broken window. An excellent plan but almost impossible to do.

Jelly was so excited, it was hopeless trying to get her to stand any distance away from him so that he could photograph her. In the end, Sam just clicked the camera at anything and everything he could see, including a bit of a tail in one shot, half a foot in another and a fat wet nose in the last.

"Hurry Sam, I can hear some sort of noise from the house," came the frantic whisper from his grandmother. Sam bent down, picked up the dog and shoved its squirming body through the broken window. Unfortunately, a shard of glass remaining in the frame slashed her skin as she went.

"OWW, Oww, Oww, Jelly howled in pain and continued to howl.

"**Shur up, shur up Dog**!" came the bellow from the house. The back door flew open and a figure was silhouetted in the light from the kitchen. To her horror

Gran saw Marko. He was still there; Marko, six foot three inches tall, and very angry.

Chapter 15

The Third Question

"Shur' up! Shur' up dog!"

Marko bellowed again from the doorway, but Grandmother was there, she had snipped the cable and the lights fizzled out.

"Fuse gone! Not again! Where are the spares…?" Sam felt nothing, thought nothing and just acted without knowing how he had done it. He leaped through the window. His grandmother, the shopping bag and the dog had gone, and within seconds he had joined them, first in the bushes below the wall and then over the wall. It was only then that he realized that his face was sticky and salty stuff was running into his mouth.

It had to be blood.

"The car's on the road!" hissed his grandmother. A minute later they had reached the road and there stood the Colonel's ancient Morris Oxford. "When little problems flare up, he lets me drive it," she declared, as all three of them bundled themselves into the front seats. "I think we should go straight to hospital. You have blood running into your ear."

At the accident and emergency department of the local hospital his grandmother declared calmly, "He fell through a glass door – playing silly games with his dog. Do you stitch up dogs as well?"

Sam heard the nurse mutter, 'Batty old woman!' as she strode off. After an hour's wait Sam was stitched up, but not until he finally got home with the five stitches down his cheek, did he begin to feel a dull throbbing pain.

Luckily, Jelly's wounds were only surface scratches, except for her poor mutilated ear. They had washed her ear, very gently, in warm water, and that was all that they could think of doing for it. It had stopped bleeding and just looked messy. And Jelly was so happy to be home. Her injuries did not seem to upset her.

Sitting up in bed Sam told his grandmother everything that had happened that day, and she told him that she had made £150 profit on the sale of her marmalade.

"Gran?"

"Yes?"

"I've worked something out."

"Mmm?"

"It's being afraid of things that stops you doing anything. If you just start to do what you have to do, then it's just little decisions, one after another, and suddenly you've done that big thing you were scared of."

Gran nodded, "You mean like deciding you just had to go through the wood? Well, life's like that all the time." Not a bad day, all in all, they agreed between themselves. Jelly was stretched full length across Sam's bed, her wet nose inches from Sam's pillow. She was snoring gently but her half-closed eyes were fixed on his face. Sam slid lower down under the covers so that his face was level with Jelly's.

His grandmother switched on the nightlight he used to have when he was little and turned the CD player on to a very quiet volume, as she slipped out of the room. 'L'aprés-midi d'un faune' played out into his dappled bedroom.

On Sunday afternoon, when the Colonel had come back they both went for tea with him, and recounted a highly dramatic account of the rescue of Jelly from her prison. He told them to gather together the original kidnap letter with its horrible attachment of a bit of Jelly's ear, and the photographs Sam had taken of the inside of the garage. Then they both wrote an honest and straightforward account of what they themselves had done, and why. All this would be left at a local solicitor's office, together with the film of the previous attack on Sam by Toughie, Spike and Jaz, so that should trouble arise again they would have positive evidence of what had been happening.

It was two nights later he had another dream. It had been one of those dreams where things never, ever, go right. He had been in some huge airport, all on his own, and he was trying to arrange a special ticket for a special flight from a special country for a special person, so he ran from desk to desk saying… 'Please, please give me the ticket,' but nobody really listened to him. Every few seconds some one said: '**He**'s **ne**arly **ar**ranged it,' then he would run to another horrible crowded part of the airport and find that what he had tried to organise had not worked out. Finally he had woken up, tired and grumpy.

He Ne Ar

He nearly **ar**ranged it, but what? What was he supposed to arrange?

Then one evening just a few days later, he discovered what it all meant. His Dad had been scheduled to return home and as both his grandmother and Lucy were out at a cookery evening class, Sam had walked Jelly and then wandered back to his dad's flat, expecting him to be home by then. When he was nearly there, he noticed that the daylight was a funny colour, a strange greenish yellow. Then he let himself into the flat and saw the answer phone flashing.

"Hallo Sam, this is Caroline," one of the women who worked with his father. "Horrendous fog over Heathrow Airport. We hoped to be able to land at Luton, but we have had to redirect to Dublin and I have no idea when we will finally get in. So your dad says you are to go back to your grandmother's. OK? And he should be back tomorrow. Bye."

Sam stared out of the window. Grey fog, thick and sticky as mushroom soup, was making everything blurred and indistinct. It would be horrible to walk through that smudgy yellow air.

He would stay put; it was warm and safe in the flat. There was always plenty of food in the freezer, he knew how to lock up, how to manage everything. He wouldn't tell anyone, so no one would be worried.

It was a bit quiet, but he got himself some tea and curled up on the sofa. He was about to switch on the TV when he suddenly realised that he still had the little velvet bag with the scrap of shiny paper, in his trouser pocket.

He pulled the bag from his pocket and fished out the paper…

He Ne Ar

The light shining from the table lamp on to the paper, made the letters blur a little. He noticed that there was something else there. He twisted the paper round, moving it backwards and forwards in the light of the lamp. By looking at the paper sideways, he could pick out another letter. He tried the same action with the paper another way round; yes there was another letter there. Dropping the paper down on the coffee table he searched in his schoolbag for a pen and pencil. After a few minutes he had discovered three extra pairs of letters:

Kr Xe Rn

Six pairs of letters not three:

He Ne Ar Kr Xe Rn

But what about the dream, he had only dreamt that funny phrase about three pairs of letters…

He nearly **ar**ranged it.

There had been no words with **Kr**, or **Xe** and **Rn** in them and anyhow, what word has **Xe** in it?

And he had to think; the dream had suggested first of all:

'**He ne**arly **ar**ranged… something?' So was the arrangement supposed to have something to do with the next lot of letters:

Kr Xe Rn? It had to make some sort of sense – but what?

In desperation, he got up and wandered around the flat, just to try and get his stupid mind to work out something. It was a good half-hour later when he thought of the computer: the Internet: the World Wide Web. Perhaps, just perhaps, if he joined the pairs of letters together, they might mean something.

They didn't.

He typed: '**henearkrxern**' and '**henear**'. Then he tried '**hen ear**'. There were some wonderful 'hen ear' entries on the web, all about real hen's real ears, but they didn't help. Next he tried '**krxern**' and by accident, he stumbled on something. In his rush, he found he had tapped in '**krxe**' and it came up as a website.

Seconds later he had a picture on his screen of a small delicate ballet dancer, belonging to the Moldavian Ballet Company. Her name was **Kr**istianna **Xe**ndoxa, **Kr**...**Xe**, and she had flaming dark red curly hair.

Kristianna.

He knew the name Kristianna already.

It was scribbled in green ink on the inside of half a dozen of his father's books. Kristianna; no Xendoxa, just Kristianna.

Sam sat still for a long time, looking at the picture, and slowly sorting the words in his mind.

'**He ne**arly **ar**ranged **Kr**istianna **Xe**ndoxa ......**rn**'

What was the '**rn**'? Was it reunion? Was it return?

Yes, it could be: 'He nearly arranged Kristianna Xendoxa's return.' He was positive now. He remembered his dream about trying to arrange a ticket at the airport.

The 'he' was his father, the 'Kristianna Xendoxa', was someone who his father had known really well. After all, he had her books; she had written her name on the inside cover; she must have been his friend. Perhaps she had left and his father had tried to 'arrange' her 'return', but had not managed it. And she had red hair.

Then slowly, slowly he walked to the mirror, and gazed at his small, faintly freckled face, and his thatch of dark, curly red hair. His hair, which if they allowed him to grow long, would fly out in all directions, just like the ballet dancer's.

Then slowly, so slowly (because he was both afraid and excited) he walked into his father's bedroom, to a big filing cabinet, which he kept in one corner. The top drawer was labelled 'WORK'. The second draw was labelled 'FINANCES' and the bottom drawer, 'PERSONAL'.

There was a big fat file for 'SAMUEL JEFFERY ROBERTS'. Sam took it out, opened it up, leafed through and found what he was looking for. He found his birth certificate.

Mother's name? Kristianna Xendoxa. He had the

answer to his third question: the one he had never dared to ask anyone.

Chapter 16

The Shining Letters

He had a mother.

He walked even more slowly back to the sofa. He had a mother; she had red hair like him, she was small like him, her name was Kristianna Xendoxa and she was a ballet dancer with the Moldavian ballet Company. He suddenly remembered how, when they had reached the pub beside the canal, they had seen a huge hoarding advertising a show featuring the Moldavian ballet Company.

At that moment the phone screamed through the empty flat. "Sam!" it was Lucy, "I'm back with your grandmother and we have just watched the news: all planes have been grounded. Is Dad back?"

Sam didn't answer, but finally he muttered, "Well, not exactly."

"You're there on your own?" she was shouting.

"Sort of." There was a chattering going on between his grandmother and Lucy.

"We've worked it out: Beryl will walk over to you, the two of you will walk to the Colonel's, and then all three of you will walk here, OK?"

"It's foggy out there. How will you all get home?" Sam protested. He didn't want all these people to be stumbling around in the darkness of the fog, because of him.

"Oh, you should just see the bedding your grandmother is dragging out of cupboards. We will all stay here for the night. Get the Colonel to bring some eggs and bacon. And let your dad know you are safe."

He put the phone down and rang the emergency number that he had for his dad. "Oh, Sam," It was Caroline. "So glad to hear from you. Your dad has been worried sick. He got no answer from your grandmother's."

"It's alright," he answered, tears dripping into the corners of his mouth, (why was he crying?) "The rest of the family have sort of rescued me. Tell him not to worry." 'The rest of the family'; he'd said it almost without thinking.

While he was waiting for Beryl to arrive, he knew there were all sorts of ends, which would need tying up, but they weren't really important. He had the answer to his third question; the one about his mother and he had discovered along the way, a most amazing family: Grandmother, Dad, The Colonel, Lucy, Beryl, even Spitfire; she was like a big sister. He would have to find out why Kristianna Xendoxa had come and then gone, but right at this moment he was actually looking forward to the journey through the mysterious fog-filled town.

The sleeping arrangements were very simple: anyone over seventy was to sleep in a bed, anyone under seventy was to sleep on the floor. Next morning, when Sam woke up wedged in a small cosy corner between the back of the sofa and the wall, Lucy and Beryl had already left for work, Grandmother was down at the flower market and the spring sunshine was streaming in through the kitchen window. Winter was over. The Colonel was quietly frying eggs and bacon, and from the smell in the kitchen, had been doing so for some time.

"Breakfast, young man?" he enquired cheerily, as Sam ambled through the door. He was just about to answer, when the phone hanging on the wall next to him rang.

"Hello? …Oh hello Spitfire, did you try my dad's first?"

"Yes, and then I presumed you must be there. Listen, I know what all those letters mean. I tried to catch you after school but you had whipped off really quickly. We did it in science."

"Did what?"

"Did those letters; they are all in the Periodic Table, and our teacher said this thing: 'the periodic table explains the family relationships between all the different elements in the natural world.' "

"But why are they letters and not proper names?"

"Oh, they are like nicknames, so that last three you found...**He Ar Ne**: that's Helium, Argon and Neon."

"OK," said Sam slowly, "Are the next three **Kr**, **Xn** and **Rn**?"

"Wait a minute, I'll have to look at the sheet he gave us for homework... hang on... yes... that's right. They are **Kr Xn Rn**: that means Krypton, Xenon and Radon. How did you know those were the next ones in that family?"

"Tell you later Spitfire, I've got eggs and bacon waiting for me."

"Lucky you! I had porridge."

He put down the phone. The plate of eggs and bacon was there on the table, and the Colonel was sitting on the other side with a huge mug of steaming coffee. Sam ate every scrap of food on his plate, put down his knife and fork and said slowly:

"The periodic table?"

"**Be Mg Ca Sr Ba Ra**," murmured the Colonel.

"**Be**ryllium, **M**agnesium, **C**alcium, **S**trontium, **B**arium, **R**adium." He paused for a moment, made a funny little grin and said, "Beryl the Magnificent Calling Srangles Barking Rapidly."

"And **H Li Na K**?"

"Not so easy; but it goes, **H**ydrogen, **Li**thium, the **Na** is Sodium, (the old-fashioned name was **Na**trum) and **K** is Potassium (the old name was **K**ali). So the nicknames are **H Li Na K**, or High Lindly's Natural Karate."

"And **B C N O F**?"

"Really easy those: **B**oron, **C**arbon, **N**itrogen, **O**xygen and **F**luorine. You can see how that became '**B**ack of the **C**anal **N**ext to an **O**pen **F**ield'."

"All my fantastic letters on pieces of shiny paper were really just a bit of chemistry," spluttered Sam in disgust; the disappointment dragging down the corners of his mouth, his own little bit of magic was evaporating before his eyes. His wonderful mysterious letters; the dreams they built, the shining paper...

"Chemistry can be fantastic," said the Colonel quietly. "And the way all those parts interlock is fantastic. The man, Dmitri Ivanovich Mendeléev, who discovered the periodic table, showed how all the elements in the world had their own special families."

" Really?" this was a new idea to Sam, "But how was it that I found those scraps of lovely paper with the letters on them?" Sam was still not totally convinced, "and how did they magic themselves into dreams?"

The Colonel got up and walked to the window, then walked slowly back, "Somebody asked me to lead you into an adventure; it started out as a sort of paper chase but then it seemed to develop a life of its own. We planted those slips of paper where we hoped you would find them. I and your father. We wanted it to be a mystery quest specially for you." Sam pictured his father and the Colonel creeping around in the wet undergrowth, trying to find good hiding places.

"I had worked on a programme called *Sleep Induced Learning,* **SIL** for short. You bury words into a musical CD. The music plays and the person listening to it, learns a sequence of words. We were using it to speed up language tuition for our intelligence agents."

"Spies?" asked Sam with amazement.

"Something like that," agreed the Colonel. "That,

of course, is what Mr. Wilson stole from my computer. However, I still can't work out how Spitfire and Toughie somehow got hold of the same CD and so dreamed the same dream as you did."

Sam knew. He had been asked to take to school, a favourite piece of music. He had just shoved a CD into his school bag that morning. Maybe the entire class had actually dreamt those words 'back of the canal next to an open field' that night.

Sam took a deep breath, "What about Kristianna Xendoxa, and who was it that asked you to organise this quest for me?"

"Kristianna! Oh lovely Kristianna. She emailed me about a year ago and suggested this discovery trail."

He paused for a moment, rubbing the back of his head, " It was meant to lead you in all sorts of different directions and finally to her, but we hadn't bargained for the Wilson family. That lot almost dislodged the whole quest."

He stopped again, looking out of the window, and then started up, almost talking to himself, "Your father met Kristianna when he worked in Moscow. She is like a humming bird; beautiful, kind, exciting, but there was no way anyone could pin her down. She tried to be a good mother to you, but it nearly drove her mad, so your grandmother stepped in. And Kristianna returned to her ballet." Then the Colonel did something he had never done before: he stretched out his hand, his old hand, skinny with wrinkled blue veins and for just a few seconds laid it protectively over the back of Sam's.

"We all miss her, she was a burst of sunshine. She got all those gorgeous bits of paper for me." And there were tears in his eyes.

"My box: the lacquer box, the one with all those bright colours and pictures of a sort of prince and princess, was that my mum's? It's got to J.R. from K.X. on it."

"Good heavens I didn't know you had it; yes your mother gave that to your father. It is very valuable."

"I kept all the shining scraps in it." Sam told him.

"Oh, when you email her, you will have to tell her that." Email; he could email his mother. That was good.

"So, Sam, no more questions?" said the Colonel, gathering up the plates. Sam paused, only a split second but the Colonel noticed, "What?"

"It's like this," he was stumbling over his words, "Dad is so busy, and Gran, well she should be having a rest and, well, …please… be honest, ...am I a nuisance?" He looked down at his hands, at the floor, anywhere but at the Colonel's face.

There was a long slow breath, a sort of snort of air from the Colonel, "Your dad loves you, your gran loves you, I love you, Lucy loves you, Beryl loves you, Spitfire thinks you are her best friend; you fill up a great empty gap in all our lives."

"Well, I suppose that's alright then," Sam replied, smiling slowly, "I think I'll take Jelly for a run." He stood up, grinned at the Colonel and said, "I suppose she isn't a Sranglehund either?"

"Ah, now: as far as we can say for certain, her mother was a Deutscher Langharriger Vorsteh Hund, and her father? Well, he could have been an orange-haired orang-utan, as far as we know."

"A Deutscher Langharriger Vorsteh Hund," said Sam happily as he went to collect her lead, "almost as good as a Sranglehund."

Writing And Publishing To Raise Money For A Good Cause

Elizabeth Dye lives in a village in Derbyshire. She has written this book and illustrated it herself to raise money for the crumbling fabric of the local church and Seven Arches Publishing is contributing to that aim by donating all profits from the sales of this book to this cause.

An Appeal by Elizabeth Dye

St Anne's Church in Ambergate has got a real problem. The steps up to the main entrance are collapsing so we want to build a disabled access ramp to replace these crumbling old steps; this will enable wheelchairs, babies' buggies, funeral parties, and everyone else to enter safely.

Competitions And Activities For Seven Arches Books

Look out for the competitions and activities on our website www.sevenarchespublishing.co.uk They are always changing, and shortly there will be some will be based on Sam's exciting adventures in this book. Also on our website, budding scientists will find information about the periodic table of elements that Spitfire tells Sam about in the last chapter. You can find out about the scientist Dmitri Mendeléev, who first arranged the elements in the table in horizontal rows; this was a very exciting discovery in 1869.

While you are there, why not have a look at our other books. The exciting story of 'Nidae's Promise'which is about a swallow, has a whole range of fun activities based on the book, or on your knowledge of birds, especially swallows. Sometimes we offer book token prizes for entries that appear on the website.

The first in our Time Travelling Kids series, a book called 'Danny Higgins Time Traveller' will run its first competition in Autumn 2009. Watch out for Danny's own page on MySpace.

Publishing With Principles

Our books for children are not only exciting adventures, they stretch and challenge them as readers and learners, and are unlikely to pander to the latest trends. Our first book, 'Nidae's Promise' encouraged wonder at the amazing life of swallows. Danny Higgins – Time Traveller, the first in our series 'The Time-Travelling Kids' celebrates the history of our nation. The Winter of Magical Letters puts encourages interest in science as Sam finds out it is science not 'magic' that has created his adventures.

We are striving to make our business a good place for people to work and to offer employment to those, who through disabilities or other reasons, have found it difficult to get work elsewhere.

Our books are generally printed in this country so that delivery is nearby and the paper used is from managed forests.

Contact Us

You are welcome to contact Seven Arches Publishing by:

Phone: 0161 612 0866

Or

Email: admin@sevenarchespublishing.co.uk